EVERY DAY,
HOLY DAY

EVERY DAY, HOLY DAY

365 *Days of Teachings and Practices*
from the Jewish Tradition of Mussar

Alan Morinis

ASSISTED BY
RABBI MICHA BERGER

TRUMPETER
Boston & London
2010

Trumpeter Books
An imprint of
Shambhala Publications, Inc.
Horticultural Hall
300 Massachusetts Avenue
Boston, Massachusetts 02115
www.shambhala.com

9 8 7 6 5 4 3 2 1

First Edition
Printed in the United States of America

⊛This edition is printed on acid-free paper that meets the
American National Standards Institute z39.48 Standard.
♻This book was printed on 30% postconsumer recycled paper.
For more information please visit www.shambhala.com.

Distributed in the United States by Random House, Inc.,
and in Canada by Random House of Canada Ltd

Designed by James D. Skatges

Library of Congress Cataloging-in-Publication Data
Every day, holy day: 365 days of teachings and practices
from the Jewish tradition of mussar/edited by
Alan Morinis; assisted by Micha Berger.
    p. cm.
ISBN: 978-1-59030-810-3 (pbk.: alk. paper)
1. Jewish devotional calendars.   2. Jewish ethics.
3. Spiritual life--Judaism.   4. Self-actualization (Psychology)—
Religious aspects—Judaism.   5. Musar movement.
        I. Morinis, E. Alan.   II. Berger, Micha.
            BM724.E95 2010
            296.7'2—dc22
            2010008307

Contents

Introduction

MUSSAR IS A JEWISH spiritual tradition that offers insight and guidance for living by directing us to pay attention to the impact that our inner traits have on our lives. The Mussar teachers take note of the Torah's teaching, "You shall be holy" (Leviticus 19:1), and find in this injunction the primary guideline for living. They perceive that each of us at our core is inherently a holy being, and the issue of living is to recognize and then to remove the obstacles to that inborn holiness. Those obstacles show up in our lives as inner traits (*middot*) that are tending toward either extreme. Those extreme qualities (which will be different for each of us) make up a personal spiritual curriculum, whether that be too much or too little patience, an excessive tendency to generosity or miserliness, rage or indifference, and so on. The path of Mussar begins with coming to awareness of the traits that are on your spiritual curriculum, and then doing the work to change those traits, to bring them back toward the mean. Mussar has developed as a perspective on life, an insightful body of knowledge about human nature, and as a path of practice, all devoted to helping each of us overcome negative tendencies, strengthen the positive, and take steps in the direction of the holy.

Mussar has its origins in the Bible itself (see, for example, Proverbs 4:13: "Hold fast to *mussar* and do not let go."). It emerged as a unique area of study in the tenth century, in the writings of the Babylonian sage Sa'adia Gaon (892–942), and developed into a path of practice in the nineteenth century. This phenomenon was known as the Mussar movement, which centered in Lithuania and was led by Rabbi Yisrael Salanter. Mussar almost disappeared from sight in the aftermath of the Holocaust, when the pathways of Jewish spiritual practice were allowed (or, in some cases, deliberately caused) to grow over and become unavailable. The teachings and ways of Mussar are now being discovered or rediscovered in all segments of the Jewish world and beyond, because the wisdom that is embodied in Mussar offers unparalleled guidance in how to live a fulfilling human life. In so many ways, the masters of Mussar got it right, as much for this generation as for previous ones.

Mussar has always been a daily practice, and so this book is organized according to that traditional format. It offers you inspiration and support as a daily companion on your spiritual journey, and marks a pathway toward the goal of Mussar study and practice, which is to uncover the innate holiness that radiates within your soul. That goal also has roots in the Bible, where we find in several places straightforward advice to make holiness the aim of our lives. "You shall be holy" (Leviticus 19:1) is how the Torah puts it, and in directing us in this way, the verse uses the plural to indicate that every individual ought to make his or her spiritual life their highest priority. As Rabbi Yechezkel Levenstein, a recent Mussar teacher put it, "A person's primary mission in this world is to purify and elevate his soul" (*Sichos Mussar,* ed. Yitzchok Kirzner, Lakewood, N.J.: Alter Yosef Gartenhaus, 2004, 12–13.5.).

Mussar teachers have sought to help us transform our lives in the way of holiness. The path they discovered lies not in any esoteric or other-worldly area, but right within the realm of our familiar inner lives—the Mussar path to holiness goes by way of the territory of anger and calmness, generosity and miserliness, trust and worry, laziness and zeal, and all the other traits that live within us. We become holy not by becoming other than who we are, but by recognizing which traits we find challenging in the realities of our lives and then mastering them.

When a person has successfully identified and balanced all his or her inner traits, the Mussar teachers say that person has become whole, or *shalem* in Hebrew. You'll notice the similarity of the word for "wholeness" and the word for "peace," the familiar *shalom.* The path of Mussar leads to holiness, wholeness, and peace.

TRAITS OF CHARACTER IN SPIRITUAL
LIFE AND GROWTH

It is a Mussar insight that we are all endowed with the full range of the inner traits, and that each trait has its place in our spiritual journey, though some are stepping-stones while others function as obstacles to holiness. Each of us has every one of the traits, though they are configured differently within each of us. Some of our traits will be in excellent shape and measure, but there are sure to be at least some that tend toward the extreme—whether in abundance or shortage—and it is those traits that tend away from the golden mean that make up our own unique spiritual pathway. To put it another way, every person has their own spiritual curriculum that consists of just those certain traits that they tend to express in excess or deficiency.

A person who is easily and often angered counts rage on their spiritual curriculum, just as the habitually stingy person has been assigned to master generosity. The impatient person has patience on his or her curriculum, and the worried person has been given an assignment to develop trust. And so it is for all of us. We all have some traits that are tending toward either extreme on the range, and our personal pathway to holiness involves cultivating the ideal within each of those traits.

When the impatient person becomes patient, or the harsh person masters kindness, or the lazy one becomes energetic, then a spiritual obstacle is lifted, and more of the light of holiness shines brightly into that person's life and, through them, into the world. Each trait that is mastered in this way brings you one step closer to being whole: *shalem;* and to knowing peace: *shalom.*

How does this transformation take place? By way of practice. Since at least the eighteenth century, the Mussar teachers have told us that only a consistent regimen of daily practice can alter our inner traits. For this purpose, they developed meditations, contemplations, visualizations, and other practices. A small dose of daily practice aimed at a particular trait has the effect of "leaving a trace on the soul," deep within. Over time, these traces accumulate until the balance on the trait is altered, and we are transformed. That tradition of daily practice gives rise to this book.

THE ORGANIZATION OF *Every Day, Holy Day*

Mussar practice calls for focusing on one trait every day for one week. Then, in the next week, you focus on a different trait for those seven days. That weekly pattern continues until all the traits on a student's list have been studied and practiced. Then the first trait on the list is taken up once again, and the whole roster is repeated.

What the student actually does on each of the days when he or she is focused on a specific trait depends on the level of experience the student has with Mussar. Everyone does some measure of study, but beyond that, the pattern of practice varies from person to person.

Every Day, Holy Day is organized according to this traditional model and provides a core Mussar practice for daily engagement. I have chosen to introduce twenty-six of the key traits in this book, though there are others that live within us and that may be important for you to master on your journey toward holiness. The twenty-six dealt with here are all very important, however, and through your engagement with them you will come to know yourself better, and you will get help to identify the qualities that are on your own personal spiritual curriculum, and you will also know what to do about them.

Every page in this book is given over to one day in the year, and each contains the following elements:

- The name of trait that is in focus that week
- An inspiring or insightful teaching from a Mussar teacher or source
- A phrase that captures the essence of what that trait is about
- A space for keeping a daily journal

When we encounter a trait for the first time, I've added a few lines of explanation to ensure that you have a clear image of which inner quality we are dealing with. Mussar definitions of the traits are very insightful and can offer new understandings of what goes on within us. The Mussar masters help us to see what is really involved in concepts such as "patience" and "humility." If you want to learn more about the specific traits, many of the ones dealt with here are given a fuller treatment in my book *Everyday Holiness*.

Three of the elements that show up on every page of this book—the phrases, the exercises, and the journaling—need a bit of explanation in order for you to use them to maximum effect.

The phrase that accompanies each trait is meant to capture the essence of that trait in words. You are given these phrases in order to set up a daily morning contemplation of the trait, so that you start your day with that day's trait firmly embedded in your consciousness. The simplest way to do this contemplation is to repeat the phrase to yourself several times. Better still is to repeat it aloud. In the nineteenth century, the practice was to repeat the phrase over and over, chanting it with a melody and allowing the heart to soar with emotion. (This is the traditional Mussar practice known as *hitpa'alut,* which is often translated as "chanting with lips aflame.") You may want to try that. I know people who every week write their phrase on a card that they keep by their bed so they see it first thing every morning. Others change the screensaver on their computer to bring up the daily phrase whenever their computer is idle. People write it on notepaper and put it on the coffeepot, or on the dashboard of the car, or on the kitchen table, wherever they are bound to intersect with it as they begin their day.

Contemplating the daily phrase raises your awareness of the day's trait. You will be amazed at the effect that extra awareness has. Not only will you see that particular trait so much more clearly as it shows up in your day, you will also be much more aware of how you yourself embody that trait, and the choices you have in how you express it.

Your daily practice also includes an exercise, which the Mussar teachers have traditionally called *kabbalot* (singular, *kabbalah*). *Kabbalot* are practical exercises that focus on the same soul-trait that you are engaged with in that week's other practices, the morning phrase and the evening journal. These *kabbalot* are meant to be very attainable, neither too much of a challenge (which can lead to failure and despair), nor too easy (in which case there will be no stretch and growth involved). If you find the assigned *kabbalot* too difficult, reduce the exercise to a level you can accomplish. If one of the *kabbalot* proves to be too easy, step up the demand on yourself. The idea is to address change in the soul-trait progressively, by succeeding in small exercises that are easier to implement, and then moving incrementally to more significant steps. The Mussar teachers tell us that it is far better to accomplish a small step successfully and consistently rather than attempting a big leap, which you may or may not make, and which can't be sustained.

Keeping a daily journal is also a traditional Mussar practice. (See the book *Cheshbon Ha'Nefesh* by Rabbi Menachem Mendel Leffin, published in 1811, for more on this practice.) Contemplating the phrase in the morning starts off the day with awareness, the exercises keep you engaged during the day, and it is best to do your journaling in the evening to record and clarify to yourself what was revealed in the light of that awareness. In that way, the journaling adds to and completes what you begin in the morning with the phrase.

When writing in the journal, record briefly anything you saw that day that demonstrated the trait of the day, including how you did on the *kabbalah* for that period. Focus as much as possible on how that trait showed up in you, and in doing so, just describe. Because the point of the practice is to fix the trait in awareness, and to develop a sense of the range of choice that is available to you in how you think and act. Don't reward yourself for instances when you behaved in ways you approve of, nor condemn yourself when you fumbled in one way or another. The journal is not an evaluation but rather a brief, factual record of the appearance of the daily trait in your life.

Mussar practice is not disconnected from the traditional Jewish practice of the commandments, one of which is not to write on the Sabbath. That does not present much of a problem, as you can make your Friday journal entry before sunset and hold off on your Saturday entry until after sunset that day.

As you stay consistent with this practice over time, you will find that the daily attention to the phrase and journal has a remarkably transformative impact on your life. This is attested to in the historical writings on Mussar, in the lives of my students, and in my own life.

In fact, your own direct and personal experience of the transformative impact of Mussar is the one testimonial for the practice that carries the most weight. As one of my early Mussar teachers put it, "Mussar is not something you learn, it is something you *do,*" and in the doing will come the experience, and that experience will, in turn, provide the most effective motivation to keep you going on your journey toward holiness.

At any point when you have tasted of the fruit that comes to you from cultivating awareness and liberating yourself from habitual thought and behavioral patterns, you may want to seek additional support for your journey. I invite you to investigate the offerings of The Mussar Institute (www.mussarinstitute.org) or to be in touch with me directly by e-mail at alan@mussarinstitute.org. It is our wish to support you, as those who have come before us on this way have been a great support to ourselves.

I wish you blessings on the journey. May you find the holy in every day.

Alan Morinis
Vancouver, 2010

EVERY DAY,
HOLY DAY

GRATITUDE

THE HEBREW TERM for gratitude translates as "recognizing the good." Myriad benefits come to us every day, but most of us find it easy to overlook them and instead focus on what we lack. This trait is an invitation to sensitize yourself to the good and to the gifts that are certain to be present in your life at every moment, even if at that same moment there happen to be difficulties.

> When Rabbi Menachem Mendel, the Kotzker Rebbe, was ready to consign old shoes to the trash, he would first wrap them in newspaper to show his gratitude.

PHRASE *Awaken to the good and give thanks.*

PRACTICE Say thank you to every person who does even the slightest thing that is helpful or beneficial to you.

JOURNAL

GRATITUDE

GRATITUDE is intellectually compelling and it is a very good trait—so why are we so often ungrateful? There are two reasons for this. The first is that a person's first impression is that everything comes by itself, and that it is all coming to him. The other reason is: when I receive good from someone and I recognize that good, I became indebted to him.

—RABBI SHLOMO WOLBE (1914–2005)

PHRASE *Awaken to the good and give thanks.*

PRACTICE Say thank you to every person who does even the slightest thing that is helpful or beneficial to you.

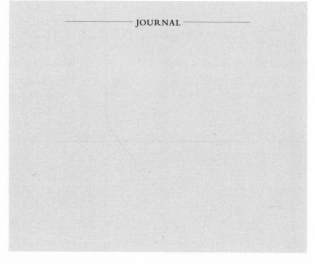

———— JOURNAL ————

WHEN YOU OPEN yourself to experience the trait of gratitude, you discover with clarity and accuracy how much good there is in your life. Practicing gratitude means recognizing the good that is already yours. If you've lost your job but you still have your family and health, you have something to be grateful for. If you can't move around except in a wheelchair but your mind is as sharp as ever, you have something to be grateful for. If you've broken a string on your violin but you still have three more, you have something to be grateful for.

—ALAN MORINIS (B. 1949)

PHRASE *Awaken to the good and give thanks.*

PRACTICE Say thank you to every person who does even the slightest thing that is helpful or beneficial to you.

——————— JOURNAL ———————

GRATITUDE

"We humans have a tendency to always want more. Therefore it is easy to forget to feel grateful and happy with the good that we already have. We should strive to feel a joy that is complete. Lack of joy with what we have is destructive both physically and spiritually."

—RABBI MORDECHAI GIFTER (1915–2001)

PHRASE *Awaken to the good and give thanks.*

PRACTICE Say thank you to every person who does even the slightest thing that is helpful or beneficial to you.

————— JOURNAL —————

"God said to Moses, 'Say to Aaron, Take your staff and stretch out your hand over the waters of Egypt and they shall become blood'" (Exodus 7:19). Why didn't Moses initiate this plague? Because the river had protected Moses when he was cast into it as an infant and his gratitude prevented him from invoking a plague against it.

—RASHI (1040–1105)

PHRASE *Awaken to the good and give thanks.*

PRACTICE Say thank you to every person who does even the slightest thing that is helpful or beneficial to you.

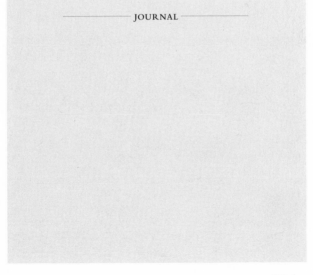

JOURNAL

GRATITUDE

ONE OF THE Ten Commandments is, "Honor your father and mother." How are we to do that? By expressing gratitude to our parents for bringing us into this world.
— *SEFER HACHINUCH* (13TH CENTURY),

PHRASE *Awaken to the good and give thanks.*

PRACTICE Say thank you to every person who does even the slightest thing that is helpful or beneficial to you.

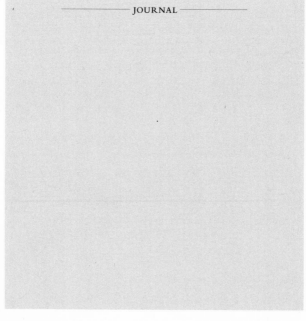

——————— JOURNAL ———————

THE MOST ELEMENTARY level of gratitude is for a person to realize that he should express gratitude—even if only with a few words—to a person who has done work for him or gone to trouble on his behalf.

—RABBI ELIYAHU DESSLER (1892–1953)

PHRASE *Awaken to the good and give thanks.*

PRACTICE Say thank you to every person who does even the slightest thing that is helpful or beneficial to you.

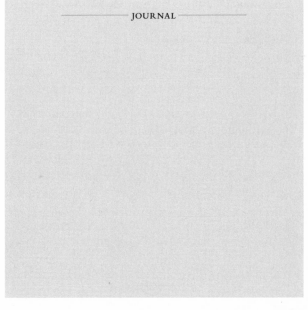

——————— JOURNAL ———————

ENTHUSIASM

SOME PEOPLE ARE energetic by nature, while others tend toward indolence. A rich person may pay to have services rendered, but there is no such bypass of laziness in spiritual matters. If you paid someone to meditate, or pray for you, then the benefit would be theirs because the effort and the experience are theirs as well. In the end, only enthusiasm for your own growth will fuel your transformation.

> Hillel would also say: If I am not for myself, who is for me? And if I am only for myself, what am I? And if not now, when?
>
> —PIRKEI AVOT 1:14

PHRASE *If not now, when?*

PRACTICE Every day, tackle one of the things that has been languishing at the bottom of your to-do list.

---JOURNAL---

ENTHUSIASM depends on the state of a person's heart. When someone frees his heart of all other thoughts that reside in it and seizes upon one thought, then he will without doubt be enthusiastic in its execution.

—*ORCHOT TZADDIKIM* (1540)

PHRASE *If not now, when?*

PRACTICE Every day, tackle one of the things that has been languishing at the bottom of your to-do list.

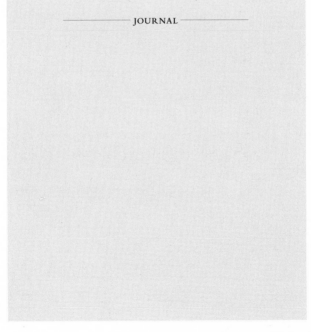

JOURNAL

ENTHUSIASM

ABRAHAM RUSHED to Sarah's tent and said, "Hurry! Three measures of the finest flour! Knead it and make rolls." Abraham ran to the cattle and chose a tender, choice calf. He gave it to a young man who rushed to prepare it.

—GENESIS 18:6–7

PHRASE *If not now, when?*

PRACTICE Every day, tackle one of the things that has been languishing at the bottom of your to-do list.

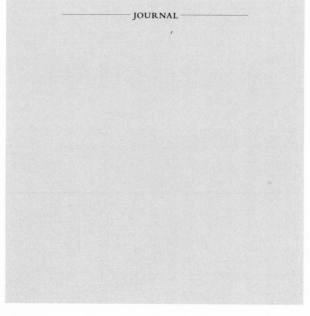

JOURNAL

JUST AS ZEAL can result from an inner burning, so can it create one. That is, one who perceives a quickening of his outer movements in the performance of a commandment conditions himself to experience a flaming inner movement, through which longing and desire will continually grow. If, however, he is sluggish in the movement of his limbs, the movement of his spirit will die down and be extinguished. Experience testifies to this.

—RABBI MOSHE CHAIM LUZZATTO (1707–1746)

PHRASE   *If not now, when?*

PRACTICE   Every day, tackle one of the things that has been languishing at the bottom of your to-do list.

——————— JOURNAL ———————

ENTHUSIASM

IT IS REPORTED that when Rabbi Simcha Zissel Ziv (1824–1898), the founder of Kelm Mussar, awoke in the morning, he would immediately spring out of his bed in great haste, as if a highwayman was standing behind him threatening to kill him—in order to overcome laziness and implant in himself the trait of enthusiasm.

PHRASE *If not now, when?*

PRACTICE Every day, tackle one of the things that has been languishing at the bottom of your to-do list.

———— JOURNAL ————

Week 2, Day 5

LAZYBONES, go to the ant; study its ways and learn. Without leaders, officers, or rulers, it lays up its stores during the summer, gathers in its food at the harvest. How long will you lie there, lazybones? When will you wake from your sleep? A bit more sleep, a bit more slumber, a bit more hugging yourself in bed, and poverty will come calling upon you, and want, like an armed soldier.

—PROVERBS 6:6–11

PHRASE *If not now, when?*

PRACTICE Every day, tackle one of the things that has been languishing at the bottom of your to-do list.

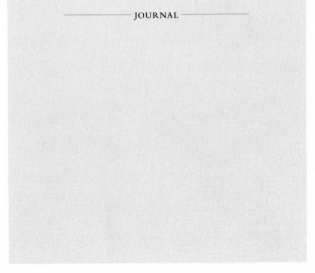

JOURNAL

MAN IS BY NATURE very "weighed down" by an earthiness and coarse materiality. That is why he does not want to exert or burden himself. But if you want to merit to divine service, you have to fight this nature and be self-motivated and enthusiastic. For if you abandon yourself to this heaviness, you will not succeed in your quest.

—RABBI MOSHE CHAIM LUZZATTO (1707–1746)

PHRASE *If not now, when?*

PRACTICE Every day, tackle one of the things that has been languishing at the bottom of your to-do list.

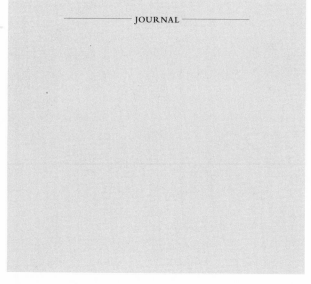

JOURNAL

JOY

—————

MOMENTS COME when the heart dances in the light. So much more than the experience of fun or even happiness, joy erupts when the inner sphere scintillates in its completeness. An experience touches us to the depths of our souls, and in that moment we are graced with a vision—if only fleetingly—of the flawless wholeness and perfection of it all. Then the heart fills and flows over, even amid the brokenness of this world.

> Light is sown for the righteous, and for the upright of heart, joy!
>
> —PSALMS 97:11

PHRASE *Mouth filled with laughter, lips with shouts of joy.*

PRACTICE Step away from your busyness and savor several moments every day; feel the joy that is available to you.

—————— JOURNAL ——————

JOY

IF ONE IS always joyful, his face will shine, his countenance will be radiant, his body will be healthy, and old age will not leap upon him, as it is written, "A happy heart is as healing as medicine" (Proverbs 17:12).

—*ORCHOT TZADDIKIM* (1540)

PHRASE *Mouth filled with laughter, lips with shouts of joy.*

PRACTICE Step away from your busyness and savor several moments every day; feel the joy that is available to you.

JOURNAL

HEAVEN AND EARTH, man and woman, soul and body—all are opposites. They aren't always opposites; there are times they influence each other positively, and there are times they reach total unity. In all connections of opposites there is joy, and it is the place and essence of joy. Anywhere joy is found there is connection or unity.

—RABBI SHLOMO WOLBE (1914–2005)

PHRASE *Mouth filled with laughter, lips with shouts of joy.*

PRACTICE Step away from your busyness and savor several moments every day; feel the joy that is available to you.

———— JOURNAL ————

ONE DAY, people noticed Rabbi Nosson Tzvi Finkel (1849–1927), the Alter of Slabodka, enjoying a private banquet. What was the occasion? He had been told that a man in a far-off land—whom he did not know—had won a great prize. So the Alter was full of joy for him. And so he made himself a party.

PHRASE   *Mouth filled with laughter, lips with shouts of joy.*

PRACTICE   Step away from your busyness and savor several moments every day; feel the joy that is available to you.

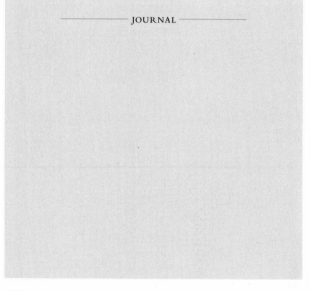

——————— JOURNAL ———————

WE VISUALIZE LIFE as but a means for joy and pleasure—as merely the medium through which to experience those fulfillments. We talk about things "worth
living for," yet in our superficial view of life, we fail
to appreciate the most profound joy of all: life itself.

—RABBI CHAIM SHMULEVITZ (1902–1979)

PHRASE *Mouth filled with laughter, lips with shouts of joy.*

PRACTICE Step away from your busyness and savor
several moments every day; feel the joy that is available to you.

——— JOURNAL ———

JOY

DELIGHT AND JOY must accompany your every spiritual endeavor. Only when you delight and rejoice in each fine and positive deed will you have the enthusiasm to act in the most ideal manner and add to your deeds every day. Only when the delight and joy in your heart are bound to your fine and positive actions will they be anchored in you.

—RABBI ABRAHAM ISAAC KOOK (1865–1935)

PHRASE *Mouth filled with laughter, lips with shouts of joy.*

PRACTICE Step away from your busyness and savor several moments every day; feel the joy that is available to you.

——————— JOURNAL ———————

IF TROUBLE COMES UPON you and you think that it has come as a punishment for a past lapse, do not be filled with guilt and despair. Rather, rejoice in this new opportunity to rise up by the medium of the test that you now face.

—RABBI DOVID BLIACHER (1891–1943)

PHRASE *Mouth filled with laughter, lips with shouts of joy.*

PRACTICE Step away from your busyness and savor several moments every day; feel the joy that is available to you.

────────── JOURNAL ──────────

STRENGTH

THE MUSSAR TEACHERS tell us that the strength that should concern us most is not that of muscles or military power, but of a spirit that can overcome all temptation to do anything but good. The necessary first step is to be aware of which inner forces pull you away from God's mountain. The greater challenge still is to apply yourself with resolute determination to overcoming those forces, so you rise ever higher on the way.

> Ben Zoma would say: "Who is mighty? One who conquers his evil inclination."
>
> —PIRKEI AVOT 4:1

PHRASE *Strong as a lion, strong as the sun.*

PRACTICE Draw very clear lines between what you will and will not do.

JOURNAL

"STRENGTH!" he would cry out to his students. "Only with strength can one pass through this world. A person who crosses a swamp in a nonchalant manner drowns. Someone who runs with all of his strength, and doesn't stop, succeeds."

—RABBI NOSSON MEIR WACHTFOGEL (1910–1998)

PHRASE   *Strong as a lion, strong as the sun.*

PRACTICE   Draw very clear lines between what you will and will not do.

―――――― JOURNAL ――――――

STRENGTH

It is well known that the three major characteristics for which people are praised in this world are: wisdom, strength, and wealth. Wisdom is the most secure of these, for it resides within a person's soul. Moreover, one's wisdom generally increases with age. Strength is next, for it resides within a person's body. However, as a person grows older, his strength generally lessens. Wealth is the least secure, for it is external.

—RABBEINU YONAH OF GERONDI (D. 1263)

PHRASE *Strong as a lion, strong as the sun.*

PRACTICE Draw very clear lines between what you will and will not do.

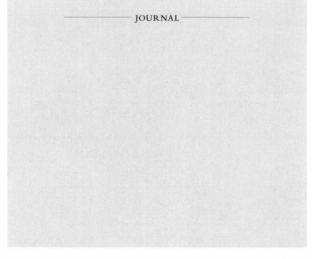

JOURNAL

WOE UNTO A PERSON who is not aware of his defects, and who does not know what he must correct. But much worse off is the person who does not know his strengths, and who is therefore unaware of the tools he must work with to advance himself spiritually.

—RABBI YERUCHAM LEVOVITZ (1873–1936)

PHRASE *Strong as a lion, strong as the sun.*

PRACTICE Draw very clear lines between what you will and will not do.

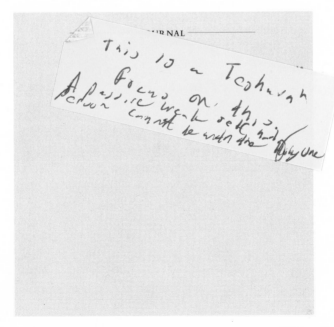

SO IT IS WITH REGARD to one's neighbors. All Israel are related one to the other, for their souls are united and in each soul there is a portion of all the others. This is the reason why a multitude carrying out the divine commands cannot be compared with the few who do so, for the multitude possesses combined strength.

—RABBI MOSHE CORDOVERO (1522–1570)

PHRASE *Strong as a lion, strong as the sun.*

PRACTICE Draw very clear lines between what you will and will not do.

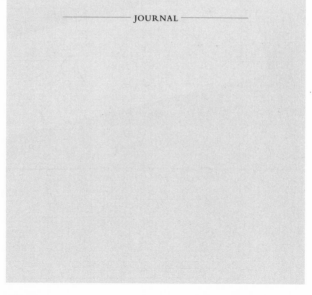

JOURNAL

THE PERSON WHO GUARDS his speech builds real power. This is the power of self-discipline, the knowledge that one has control over his impulses, that he has the inner strength to restrain himself, measure his words, and act in accord with the highest aspects of himself.

—RABBI ISRAEL MEIR KAGAN,
THE CHOFETZ CHAIM (1838–1933)

PHRASE *Strong as a lion, strong as the sun.*

PRACTICE Draw very clear lines between what you will and will not do.

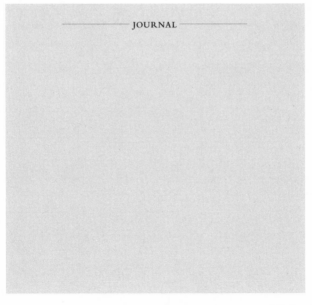

JOURNAL

STRENGTH

THE TALMUD TEACHES: "A person should always provoke his good inclination to overpower his evil inclination" (Berachot 5a). Rabbi Yerucham Levovitz (1873–1936) taught that it is a mistake to assume that the struggle between these two inner forces is one of logic, and that our actions are determined by whichever logic prevails. Not so. The battle is one of sheer force. Whichever force has the greater strength, dominates.

PHRASE *Strong as a lion, strong as the sun.*

PRACTICE Draw very clear lines between what you will and will not do.

JOURNAL

LOVING-KINDNESS

THE MUSSAR TEACHINGS tell us that the most important aspect of loving-kindness is not what you feel, but rather what you do. Our most valuable acts of loving-kindness take place when we overcome an inner resistance and do the benevolent thing anyway. It has long been understood that the heart follows the deed—do good for people, and in time your own heart is transformed into a vessel of unalloyed kindness. The other benefits, and so do we!

> The way of those who do acts of loving-kindness is to run after the poor.
> —TALMUD, SHABBAT 104A

PHRASE   *My world on selfless caring stands.*

PRACTICE   Seek out opportunities to extend active support to others, in any way that might be helpful.

JOURNAL

LOVING-KINDNESS

WHEN VISITING the home of a wealthy student, Rabbi Yisrael Salanter (1810–1883) washed his hands before eating using a minimal amount of water. His student questioned this behavior, noting that it is considered praiseworthy to wash with a generous amount. Rabbi Yisrael answered that although that is true generally, in this instance he noticed that the elderly woman working in the house was responsible for bringing the water from a distant well. While using more water would usually be preferable, in this case it would mean imposing a greater burden on this woman.

PHRASE   *My world on selfless caring stands.*

PRACTICE   Seek out opportunities to extend active support to others, in any way that might be helpful.

JOURNAL

EVE ENDED UP eating the fruit of the Tree of Knowledge because the snake fooled her, telling her that they would gain the power of Imagination and that it is the power of Imagination that gives one the God-like power of creating worlds. However, this isn't so. That ability comes from loving-kindness.

—RABBI SHLOMO WOLBE (1914–2005)

PHRASE *My world on selfless caring stands.*

PRACTICE   Seek out opportunities to extend active support to others, in any way that might be helpful.

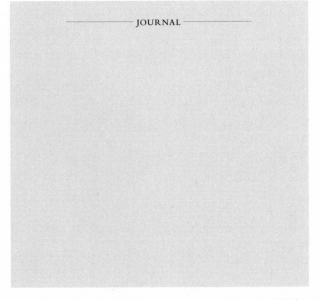

JOURNAL

RABBI SIMLAI EXPLAINED: The Torah begins with an act of loving-kindness and ends with an act of loving-kindness, as it says, "God made for Adam and his wife garments of leather and clothed them" (Genesis 3:21). It ends with an act of loving-kindness, as it says, "God buried Moses in the valley . . ." (Deuteronomy 34:6).

—TALMUD, SOTAH 14A

PHRASE *My world on selfless caring stands.*

PRACTICE Seek out opportunities to extend active support to others, in any way that might be helpful.

JOURNAL

WHEN YOU EXPERIENCE a strong desire to be good to all, realize that an illumination from the supernal world has come to you. How fortunate you will be if you prepare a proper place in your heart, in your mind, in the acts of your hands, and in all your feelings to receive this exalted guest, which is greater and more exalted than the most noble of this earth. Take hold of it and do not let go.

—RABBI ABRAHAM ISAAC KOOK (1865–1935)

PHRASE   *My world on selfless caring stands.*

PRACTICE   Seek out opportunities to extend active support to others, in any way that might be helpful.

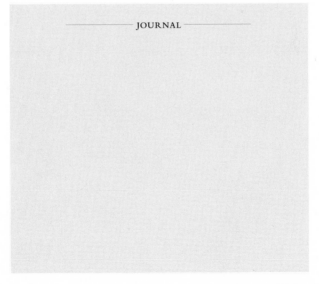

JOURNAL

LOVING-KINDNESS

FOR YEARS I THOUGHT that my ticket to the World to Come will be the *Achiezer* [his classic writings on the Torah]. Now that I am getting on in years, however, I believe that what stands in my favor is that I took responsibility for sustaining widows and orphans throughout Europe.

—RABBI CHAIM OZER GRODZINSKI (1863–1940)

PHRASE   *My world on selfless caring stands.*

PRACTICE   Seek out opportunities to extend active support to others, in any way that might be helpful.

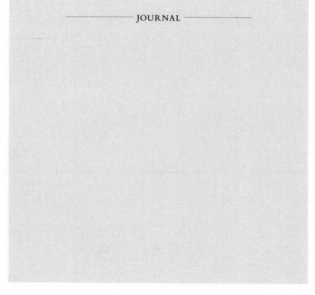

JOURNAL

OUR GREATEST DESIRE should be to do good to others, to individuals and to the masses, now and in the future, in imitation of the Creator (as it were). For everything He created and formed was according to His Will, only to be good to the creations. So, too, is it His Will that we walk in His ways.

—RABBI SHIMON SHKOP (1860–1939)

PHRASE *My world on selfless caring stands.*

PRACTICE Seek out opportunities to extend active support to others, in any way that might be helpful.

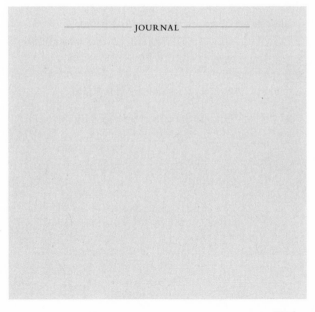

————— JOURNAL —————

ORDER

———

SO FUNDAMENTAL is the quality of order that our lives depend on it—the machines, the schedules, the systems. And the things we find beautiful are often symmetrical or proportional—all features of the trait of order. Chaos and mess are associated with disorder. At the other extreme, rigidity and obsession display an excess of order. Each of us can be a source of function and beauty, but only when we are imbued with the trait of order, tending neither to chaos nor to inflexibility.

Take time, be exact, unclutter the mind.

—RABBI SIMCHA ZISSEL ZIV,
THE ALTER OF KELM (1824–1898)

PHRASE *First things first and last things later.*

PRACTICE Set one thing in order every day this week.

——— JOURNAL ———

ALL OF YOUR ACTIONS and possessions should be orderly—each and every one in a set place and at a set
time. Let your thoughts always be free to deal with that
which lies ahead of you.

—RABBI MENACHEM MENDEL LEFFIN (1749–1826)

PHRASE   *First things first and last things later.*

PRACTICE   Set one thing in order every day this week.

——— JOURNAL ———

ORDER

IT IS EXTREMELY IMPORTANT that everyone become accustomed to order. In addition, keeping each book in its place is a great kindness, for others who will need the book will find it with ease, and will not need to waste time that should be spent in Torah study to search for it. Moreover, this is an act of respect toward the books themselves.

—RABBI ELIYAHU LOPIAN (1872–1970)

PHRASE   *First things first and last things later.*

PRACTICE   Set one thing in order every day this week.

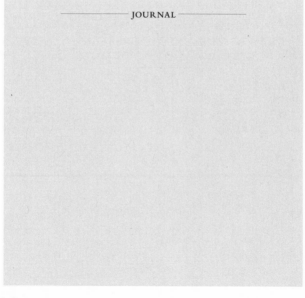

JOURNAL

WHEN WE SEE SOMEONE who is organized we know
that he must have a strong desire that motivates that
order. This applies not only to the mundane, but also to
the spiritual arena. The first step in organizing one's spiritual life is an ironclad determination. The second step is
to establish a set time for our spiritual growth in a way
that will endure, thought out and implemented with
wisdom.

—RABBI SHLOMO WOLBE (1914–2005)

PHRASE   *First things first and last things later.*

PRACTICE   Set one thing in order every day this week.

JOURNAL

ORDER

THE ALTER OF SLABODKA (1849–1927) insisted that his students conduct themselves with order. He would chastise them for leaving their hair or fingernails unattended. He would say, "A hole in one's sleeve is a hole in one's head. A wrinkled, tattered hat is a sign of confusion."

PHRASE   *First things first and last things later.*

PRACTICE   Set one thing in order every day this week.

JOURNAL

OPERATING ACCORDING to a fixed and unchanging schedule greatly aids a person's ability to manage his affairs in both worlds—in the small one [of thought] and in the larger one [of action]. This is the soul-trait of order; setting aside time for each thought and for analysis, freeing time and space for every matter in the world of action, and setting boundaries limiting each so that one not intrude upon the other.

—RABBI MENACHEM MENDEL LEFFIN (1749–1826)

PHRASE   *First things first and last things later.*

PRACTICE   Set one thing in order every day this week.

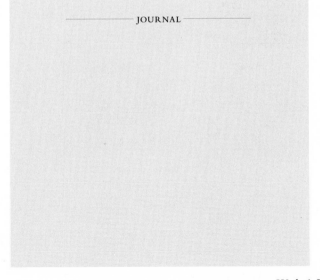

JOURNAL

ORDER

As long as a person's mind is settled, his intellectual spirit quietly stands guard, spreading its light upon his mind as if it were a torch atop the edifice of his body.

—RABBI MENACHEM MENDEL LEFFIN (1749–1826)

PHRASE   *First things first and last things later.*

PRACTICE   Set one thing in order every day this week.

JOURNAL

EQUANIMITY

———

THE HEBREW TERM that translates as "equanimity" literally means "calmness of the soul." Seeking equanimity means achieving an inner equilibrium that is not upset by the ups and downs that are part of every life. We can't insulate ourselves from life's trials, but we can prepare for them, and fostering a calm soul readies us to be the kind of people who can and will pass their life tests.

> One of the seven characteristics of a wise person is that he responds to first things first and to last things later.
> —PIRKEI AVOT 5:10

PHRASE   *Rise above the good and the bad.*

PRACTICE   When your emotions are triggered, recall that ultimate outcomes can't be predicted or controlled, and return your mind and heart to an even keel.

———— JOURNAL ————

JUST AS THE HIGH PRIEST bore the names of all the twelve tribes on the priestly garments, so do twelve principles of Mussar cast roots and establish the Mussar method. The first is that one must have peace of mind in order not to be disoriented, bewildered, or lose balance.

—RABBI YOSEF YOZEL HURWITZ,
THE ALTER OF NOVARDOK (1849–1919)

PHRASE   *Rise above the good and the bad.*

PRACTICE   When your emotions are triggered, recall that ultimate outcomes can't be predicted or controlled, and return your mind and heart to an even keel.

JOURNAL

"BECAUSE YOU SINNED, Reuben my son, the birthright was given to my son Joseph and the kingship to Judah and the high priesthood to the tribe of Levi" (Targum Onkelos to Genesis 49:3–4). Reuben was not suited to kingship or priesthood because he lacked calmness, tranquility, and peace of mind, and the clarity that goes along with it. One who acts hastily and sometimes out of confusion makes mistakes, and certainly cannot consistently make clear decisions. For success, a sense of serenity and peace of mind is required.

—RABBI MATISYAHU SALOMON (B. 1937)

PHRASE   *Rise above the good and the bad.*

PRACTICE   When your emotions are triggered, recall that ultimate outcomes can't be predicted or controlled, and return your mind and heart to an even keel.

JOURNAL

EQUANIMITY

WHY WAS THE TORAH given in the wilderness at Mount Sinai and not in the calm and peacefulness of Israel? This is to teach us that true peace of mind doesn't come from physical comforts, but from an awareness of one's ultimate life goals. When you focus on this, you are constantly traveling toward your goal and will never be overly disturbed or broken.

—RABBI YERUCHAM LEVOVITZ (1873–1936)

PHRASE   *Rise above the good and the bad.*

PRACTICE   When your emotions are triggered, recall that ultimate outcomes can't be predicted or controlled, and return your mind and heart to an even keel.

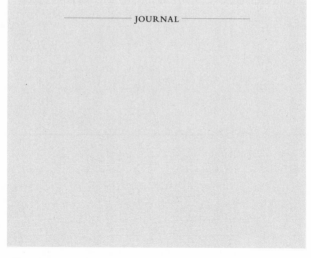

JOURNAL

Week 7, Day 4

THERE ARE FOUR TYPES of temperaments. One who is easily angered and easily appeased—his virtue cancels his flaw. One whom it is difficult to anger and difficult to appease—his flaw cancels his virtue. One whom it is difficult to anger and is easily appeased, is pious. One who is easily angered and is difficult to appease, is wicked.

—PIRKEI AVOT 5:11

PHRASE *Rise above the good and the bad.*

PRACTICE When your emotions are triggered, recall that ultimate outcomes can't be predicted or controlled, and return your mind and heart to an even keel.

———— JOURNAL ————

EQUANIMITY

PEACE OF MIND is one of the greatest pleasures a person can have; lack of peace of mind can make one's life constant torture.

—RABBI SIMCHA ZISSEL ZIV,
THE ALTER OF KELM (1824–1898)

PHRASE   *Rise above the good and the bad.*

PRACTICE   When your emotions are triggered, recall that ultimate outcomes can't be predicted or controlled, and return your mind and heart to an even keel.

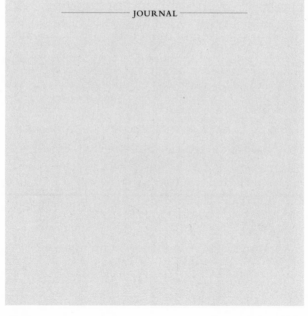

JOURNAL

A TRAVELER ARRIVED in Frankfurt and realized that he had lost his wallet. He went to Rabbi Avraham Abish Lissa, the local rabbi, who reassured him, "Don't worry, your money will be found. But first, recite the morning prayers." While praying, the man suddenly remembered where he had left his wallet. When he happily informed the rabbi that the money was found, the rabbi replied, "Of course you found it! I told you to pray because prayer restores your composure, giving you the peace of mind to remember what you had forgotten."

—ADAPTED FROM RABBI AVROHOM
CHAIM FEUER (B.1946)

PHRASE   *Rise above the good and the bad.*

PRACTICE   When your emotions are triggered, recall that ultimate outcomes can't be predicted or controlled, and return your mind and heart to an even keel.

JOURNAL

Week 7, Day 7

HONOR

EVERY HUMAN BEING is due honor and respect just by virtue of being human, which means embodying a divine soul, made in the image and likeness of God. Because we are only human, we are scarred and marred, but those are superficial blemishes. Look deeper, and you will perceive the glowing radiance of a holy soul. Develop eyes to see the soul, and bow down in honor.

> So great is the honor of created beings that concern for honor overrides even a negative prohibition promulgated by the rabbis.
>
> —TALMUD, BERACHOT 19B

PHRASE *Every one, holy soul.*

PRACTICE Make a conscious effort to greet everyone whom you encounter, before they greet you.

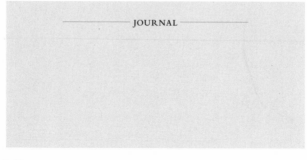

JOURNAL

A PERSON IS OBLIGATED to say, "The world was created for me" (Talmud, Sanhedrin 37a). We are obligated to be aware of our own greatness. Feel proud that you are created in the image of God. Pride in the awareness of the greatness and elevation of your soul is not only proper, but it is actually an obligation. It is a binding duty to recognize your virtues and to live with this awareness.

—RABBI AVRAHAM GRODZINSKI (1883–1944)

PHRASE   *Every one, holy soul.*

PRACTICE   Make a conscious effort to greet everyone whom you encounter, before they greet you.

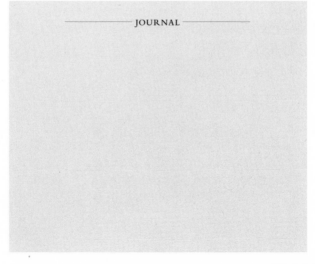

JOURNAL

HONOR DESTROYS both the body and the soul. It is disgraceful for me to be addressed as, "Our master and teacher," since I am neither. I wish to be addressed only as, "The one who loves us and seeks our good." I think that might be the truth.

—RABBI SIMCHA ZISSEL ZIV,
THE ALTER OF KELM (1824–1898)

PHRASE *Every one, holy soul.*

PRACTICE Make a conscious effort to greet everyone whom you encounter, before they greet you.

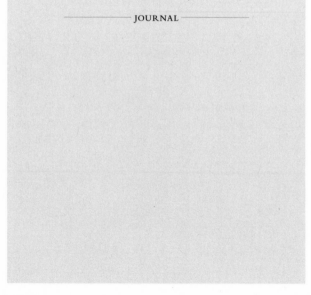

JOURNAL

BEN AZZAI would also say: Do not scorn any man, and do not discount any thing. For there is no man who has not his hour, and no thing that has not its place.

—PIRKEI AVOT 4:2

PHRASE *Every one, holy soul.*

PRACTICE Make a conscious effort to greet everyone whom you encounter, before they greet you.

——————— JOURNAL ———————

Rabbi Eliyahu Dessler treated his students with the utmost respect. When they came to visit him, he would exclaim, "What an honor that you came to visit me." Then he would take some silver cups and some wine from an old cabinet. "I made this wine myself," he would tell them, "and I only take it out for my most important guests."

—RABBI DOV WEIN (20TH CENTURY)

PHRASE *Every one, holy soul.*

PRACTICE Make a conscious effort to greet everyone whom you encounter, before they greet you.

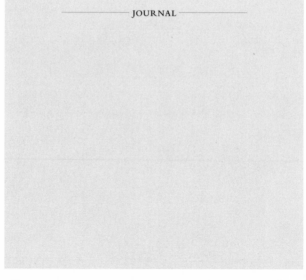

JOURNAL

ONE WHO LEARNS from his fellow a single chapter, or a single law, or a single verse, or a single saying, or even one letter—must treat the teacher with honor.

—PIRKEI AVOT 6:3

PHRASE *Every one, holy soul.*

PRACTICE Make a conscious effort to greet everyone whom you encounter, before they greet you.

JOURNAL

WHENEVER RABBI TARFON's mother wanted to go to bed, he would bend over and let her climb over him; and when she would get down, he would let her step down on him. When he told the other scholars what he did, they told him, "You still haven't reached even half the level of honor due to her."

—TALMUD, KIDDUSHIN 30B

PHRASE *Every one, holy soul.*

PRACTICE Make a conscious effort to greet everyone whom you encounter, before they greet you.

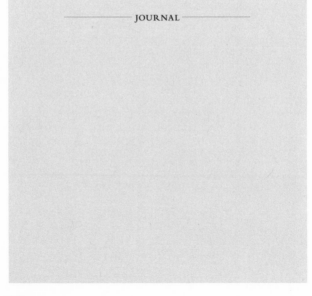

JOURNAL

HUMILITY

—————

THE EGO PROVIDES the lens through which we see all of life. If our lens is clean, we see clearly and can interact in a true way. To be arrogant or self-deprecating distorts our approach to life. Humility stands on a foundation of self-esteem, and is defined by how much space you occupy—being humble means occupying your rightful space, where "space" can be physical, verbal, emotional, financial, and so on.

> A small deed done in humility is a thousand times more acceptable to God than a great deed done in pride.
> —*ORCHOT TZADDIKIM* (1540)

PHRASE *No more than my space, no less than my place.*

PRACTICE Carry two notes in your pocket. On one, write, "I am dust and ashes"; on the other, "The world was created for me."

——————— JOURNAL ———————

CONCEIT IS COMPARABLE to a mansion that someone filled with straw. The house had holes in it and the straw would fall into the holes. After some days, the straw in those holes would fall out, and everyone would see it's just a barn full of straw.

—MIDRASH BAMIDAR RABBAH, 18:17

PHRASE   *No more than my space, no less than my place.*

PRACTICE   Carry two notes in your pocket. On one, write, "I am dust and ashes"; on the other, "The world was created for me."

———————— JOURNAL ————————

ONE WHO CRAVES ATTENTION from others has not yet found himself. He is unaware of his true worth. Lacking self-esteem, he relies on the opinion of others. He hungers for their praise, because without hearing their appreciation he feels worthless. When people do not applaud him, he feels helpless and, consequently, hostile and angry.

—RABBI SHLOMO WOLBE (1914–2005)

PHRASE *No more than my space, no less than my place.*

PRACTICE Carry two notes in your pocket. On one, write, "I am dust and ashes"; on the other, "The world was created for me."

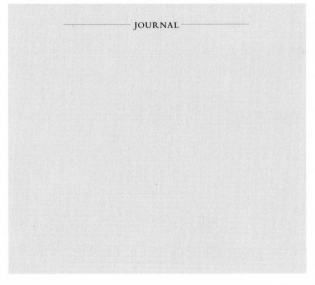

JOURNAL

HUMILITY IS ASSOCIATED with spiritual perfection. When humility effects depression it is defective. When it is genuine, it inspires joy, courage, and inner dignity.

—RABBI ABRAHAM ISAAC KOOK (1865–1935)

PHRASE *No more than my space, no less than my place.*

PRACTICE Carry two notes in your pocket. On one, write, "I am dust and ashes"; on the other, "The world was created for me."

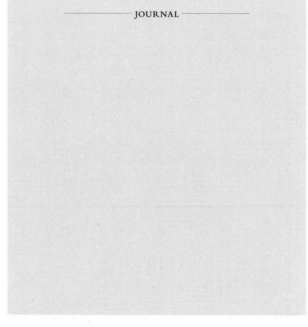

JOURNAL

PRIDE GOES BEFORE RUIN, arrogance before failure. Better to be humble and among the lowly than to share spoils with the proud.

—PROVERBS 16:18–19

PHRASE *No more than my space, no less than my place.*

PRACTICE Carry two notes in your pocket. On one, write, "I am dust and ashes"; on the other, "The world was created for me."

―――――――― JOURNAL ――――――――

HUMILITY

THE VIRTUE THAT IS REQUIRED for oneself is the diametric opposite of that which one is required to exercise in relation to others. This is particularly true concerning humility, which is the sublimest of all traits. A person is required to exercise it to the utmost degree. On the other hand, one should not treat one's fellow with this trait and degrade his status in the name of humility.

—RABBI YISRAEL SALANTER (1810–1883)

PHRASE *No more than my space, no less than my place.*

PRACTICE Carry two notes in your pocket. On one, write, "I am dust and ashes"; on the other, "The world was created for me."

JOURNAL

WHEN I GET TO HEAVEN, they'll ask me, why didn't you learn more Torah? And I'll tell them that I wasn't bright enough. Then they'll ask me, why didn't you do more kind deeds for others? And I'll tell them that I was physically weak. Then they'll ask me, why didn't you give more to charity? And I'll tell them that I didn't have enough money for that. And then they'll ask me: If you were so stupid, weak, and poor, why were you so arrogant? And for that, I won't have an answer.

—RABBI RAFAEL OF BARSHAD (1751–1827)

PHRASE *No more than my space, no less than my place.*

PRACTICE Carry two notes in your pocket. On one, write, "I am dust and ashes"; on the other, "The world was created for me."

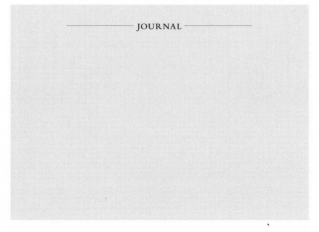

JOURNAL

GENEROSITY

THE HEART GIVES FREELY when it realizes that it is not a separate and isolated entity, but rather belongs to larger wholes. Giving comes easily to such a heart because it experiences no rupture between the one who gives and the one who receives. This may be an ideal, but in truth all acts of giving build and strengthen bonds. Generosity by its nature draws closer the giver and the receiver, until ultimately there is neither "me" nor "you," but only love.

> How goodly is this good trait of a generous spirit.
> It is a gift from God and ingrained in humanity.
> —RABBI ELIEZER PAPO (1785–1826)

PHRASE *The generous heart gives freely.*

PRACTICE Do three generous acts per day: one with your money, one with your time, one with your caring.

———— JOURNAL ————

THE GIVER GETS MORE than the recipient. The recipient acquires something material and limited. The one who gives, however, acquires for himself a good and pure heart.

—RABBI YOSEF YOZEL HURWITZ,
THE ALTER OF NOVARDOK (1849–1919)

PHRASE *The generous heart gives freely.*

PRACTICE Do three generous acts per day: one with your money, one with your time, one with your caring.

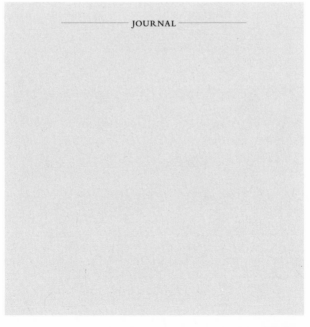

JOURNAL

GENEROSITY

GENEROSITY is the bestowal of good upon one who has no claim or entitlement to it. To pay a worker his wages or a creditor his debt is not generosity, but fairness and justice. However, giving charity to the poor, bringing guests into the home, and bestowing gifts are acts of generosity.

—RABBI AVRAHAM BEN HARAMBAM (1186–1237)

PHRASE *The generous heart gives freely.*

PRACTICE Do three generous acts per day: one with your money, one with your time, one with your caring.

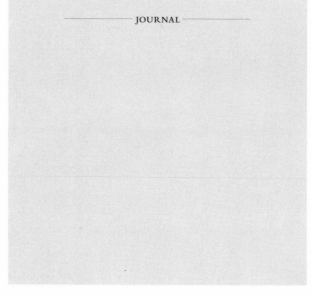

JOURNAL

INVITING IN GUESTS, people who are God's creations and children, is an even greater sign of our love of God than actually receiving the Divine Presence itself (Talmud, Shabbat 127a). If we love God so much, we are always ready to open up our homes to God's children. This is why inviting in guests is greater than receiving the Divine Presence.

—RABBI SHALOM NOACH BEREZOVSKY (1911–2000)

PHRASE *The generous heart gives freely.*

PRACTICE Do three generous acts per day: one with your money, one with your time, one with your caring.

JOURNAL

GENEROSITY

A PERSON who redeems one captive with a hundred gold coins or gives a hundred gold coins as charity to one poor person cannot be compared to one who redeems ten captives or covers the needs of ten poor people by giving ten gold coins to each. About this our Sages have said: "All is according to the preponderance of deed" (Pirkei Avot 3:15). They did not say "according to the size of the deed."

—*ORCHOT TZADDIKIM* (1540)

PHRASE *The generous heart·gives freely.*

PRACTICE Do three generous acts per day: one with your money, one with your time, one with your caring.

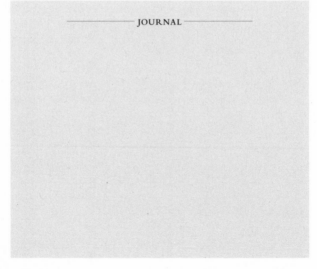

JOURNAL

A MAN CAME TO THE Brisker Rav, Yitzchak Zev So-loveitchik (1886–1959), before Passover and asked, "Is it permitted to use milk instead of wine for the Four Cups" that are drunk at the ritual meal? The rabbi took five rubles from his pocket and gave them to the man. The rabbi's wife asked, "Wouldn't one ruble have been enough for him to buy wine?" "Perhaps," responded the rabbi, "but from his question, it was clear that he didn't have money for meat either, for one can't eat meat and use milk for the Four Cups. Therefore, I gave him enough money for both meat and wine for his Passover meal."

PHRASE   *The generous heart gives freely.*

PRACTICE   Do three generous acts per day: one with your money, one with your time, one with your caring.

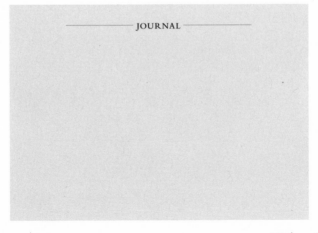

JOURNAL

GENEROSITY

THAT WHICH A PERSON GIVES to another person is never lost. It is an extension of his own being. He can see a part of himself in the one to whom he has given. This is the attachment between one person and another to which we give the name "love."

—RABBI ELIYAHU DESSLER (1892–1953)

PHRASE *The generous heart gives freely.*

PRACTICE Do three generous acts per day: one with your money, one with your time, one with your caring.

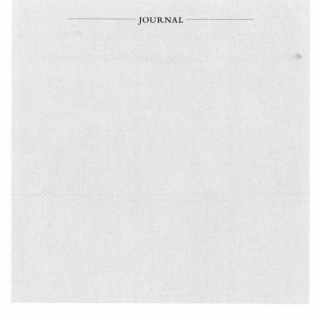

JOURNAL

WATCHFULNESS

THE HEBREW *zehirut* is often translated as "watchful-ness," or "caution." In fact, the core meaning of the term is "shining." What's the connection between a watchful awareness and the quality of "shining"? The answer is that one can only be cautious if one is endowed (or endows oneself) with a brightly shining inner awareness. It is the quality of radiant consciousness that enables a person to be vigilant about the large and the small details that make all the difference on the path of a life.

Wise ones, be watchful of your words.

—PIRKEI AVOT 1:11

PHRASE *Bright light of mind on the steps ahead.*

PRACTICE Consider for a moment the likely outcome of every action before you take it.

JOURNAL

WATCHFULNESS

FEAR IS COMPLETE foolishness. A person must not be afraid, but only needs to be careful.

—RABBI ABRAHAM ISAAC KOOK (1865–1935)

PHRASE *Bright light of mind on the steps ahead.*

PRACTICE Consider for a moment the likely outcome of every action before you take it.

JOURNAL

ONE OF THE RULES of caution is not to be too cautious.
—RABBI BAHYA IBN PAQUDA (11TH CENTURY)

PHRASE *Bright light of mind on the steps ahead.*

PRACTICE Consider for a moment the likely outcome of every action before you take it.

———————— JOURNAL ————————

IN THE MUSSAR yeshiva of Kelm, the garbage cans were designed to train students in the trait of caution. They used a tall, narrow waste bin that was prone to tumbling over. Whoever was not careful in disposing of his waste caused it to fall over and was obliged to gather up all the garbage that scattered about.

PHRASE *Bright light of mind on the steps ahead.*

PRACTICE Consider for a moment the likely outcome of every action before you take it.

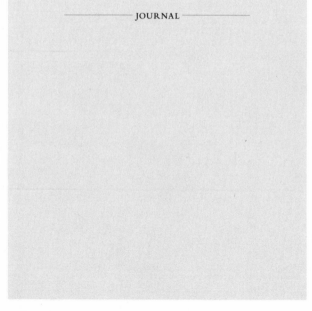

JOURNAL

KEEP YOUR HEART with all vigilance, for from it flow the springs of life.

—PROVERBS 4:23

PHRASE *Bright light of mind on the steps ahead.*

PRACTICE Consider for a moment the likely outcome of every action before you take it.

JOURNAL

WATCHFULNESS

A PERSON SHOULD OBSERVE all of his actions and watch over all of his ways so as not to leave himself with a bad habit or a bad trait, let alone a sin or a crime.

—RABBI MOSHE CHAIM LUZZATTO (1707–1746)

PHRASE *Bright light of mind on the steps ahead.*

PRACTICE Consider for a moment the likely outcome of every action before you take it.

JOURNAL

WATCHFULNESS brings one to enthusiasm.

—TALMUD, AVODAH ZARA 20B

PHRASE *Bright light of mind on the steps ahead.*

PRACTICE Consider for a moment the likely outcome of every action before you take it.

———— JOURNAL ————

JUDGING OTHERS FAVORABLY

MOST OF US are quick to jump to negative conclusions about other people. Yet we judge without knowing all the factors that go into their decisions. The Mussar teachers urge us to give up this (often unconscious) habit in order that we not cultivate a heart of suspicion in ourselves, nor a personal world peopled by perceived wrongdoers. Giving others the benefit of the doubt elevates both your own heart and the world in which you live.

> Hillel taught: Do not judge your fellow until you are in his place.
>
> —PIRKEI AVOT 2:4

PHRASE *There's another side to the story.*

PRACTICE Acknowledge an alternative explanation for actions you see others taking that you would ordinarily condemn.

———— JOURNAL ————

EVEN IF YOU PERSONALLY see someone wise sinning, say that perhaps he did it for the right reasons. And if it is a sin for which it is impossible to attribute to the right reasons, our Sages say: "When a wise person sins, do not assume that his guilt remains the next day, since he surely repented" (Talmud, Berachot 19a).

—RABBI YESHAIAH HOROWITZ (1570–1626)

PHRASE *There's another side to the story.*

PRACTICE Acknowledge an alternative explanation for actions you see others taking that you would ordinarily condemn.

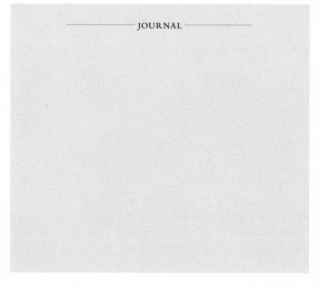

JOURNAL

THESE DAYS, GIVEN THE stresses and tension of modern life, many people are irritable and depressed. This may cause them to say things they really do not mean, and they regret having said them. We should keep this in mind and give people every consideration.

—RABBI AVRAHAM PAM (1913–2001)

PHRASE *There's another side to the story.*

PRACTICE Acknowledge an alternative explanation for actions you see others taking that you would ordinarily condemn.

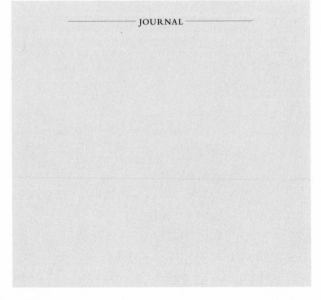

JOURNAL

ONCE A PIOUS PERSON was walking with his disciples. As they passed a dead dog, his students said, "How awful is the stench of this carcass." "How white are its teeth!" he told them; and they immediately regretted having spoken their derogatory words.

—RABBI BAHYA IBN PAQUDA (11TH CENTURY)

PHRASE *There's another side to the story.*

PRACTICE Acknowledge an alternative explanation for actions you see others taking that you would ordinarily condemn.

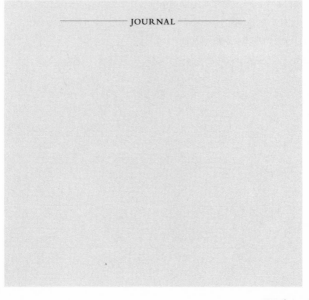

JOURNAL

JUDGING OTHERS FAVORABLY

IF YOU SEE SOMEONE who has achieved a prominent position but whose behavior is inappropriate, do not say, "If I were in his place, I wouldn't do as he does." You do not know what tomorrow will bring, and you are no different from him or anyone else. Perhaps that prestigious position would sway you as it has swayed him. Only when you reach his place and his position and overcome your own tendencies will you have the right to question his conduct.

—RABBEINU YONAH OF GERONDI (D. 1263)

PHRASE   *There's another side to the story.*

PRACTICE   Acknowledge an alternative explanation for actions you see others taking that you would ordinarily condemn.

———— JOURNAL ————

WE ARE NOT ONLY to judge favorably, but to believe in the explanations that we devise as well. What you may consider to be an absurd justification may turn out to be the truth!

—RABBI ZVI FELDMAN (1907–1976)

PHRASE *There's another side to the story.*

PRACTICE Acknowledge an alternative explanation for actions you see others taking that you would ordinarily condemn.

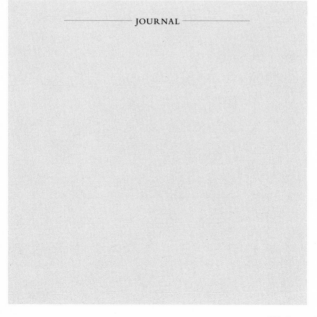

JOURNAL

ONE SHOULD NOT even think about others and their affairs unless it is for the purpose of benefiting them, whether for their bodies or their souls. Besides this, one should not think about them at all—ever.

—RABBI YISRAEL SALANTER (1810–1883)

PHRASE *There's another side to the story.*

PRACTICE Acknowledge an alternative explanation for actions you see others taking that you would ordinarily condemn.

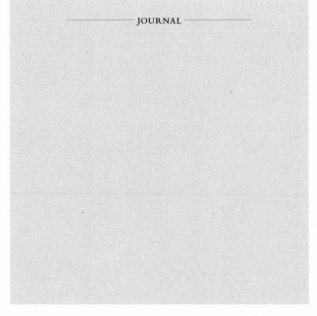

JOURNAL

CALMNESS

———

ANGER IS A POTENT inner force that everyone experiences in themselves, often followed by regret. Yet there is a positive aspect to anger—it is a signal that something you care about is endangered or wronged. How much more effective and less harmful it is when we respond not from flaming, destructive rage but from an inner place of calm and thoughtful certitude.

> The calm one is greater than a warrior, and the self-controlled is greater than a conqueror.
>
> —PROVERBS 16:32

PHRASE *Still waters of the heart.*

PRACTICE Set yourself an activity that you must do when you feel anger coming on, such as drinking a glass of water, or changing your shoes, before you permit yourself to respond.

———— JOURNAL ————

CALMNESS

KNOW THAT CALMNESS and humility are partners, just as their opposites, anger and pride, are partners. Generally, what stirs anger is inward pride, while what causes calmness is inward humility.

—RABBI AVRAHAM BEN HARAMBAM (1186–1237)

PHRASE *Still waters of the heart.*

PRACTICE Set yourself an activity that you must do when you feel anger coming on, such as drinking a glass of water, or changing your shoes, before you permit yourself to respond.

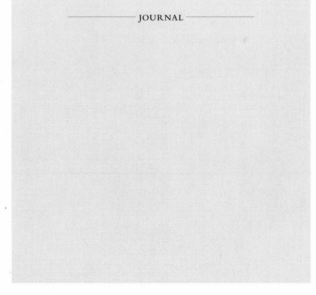

JOURNAL

REMOVE ANGER FROM your soul, and remove the evil from your flesh, for childhood and immaturity are vanity.

—ECCLESIASTES 11:10

PHRASE *Still waters of the heart.*

PRACTICE Set yourself an activity that you must do when you feel anger coming on, such as drinking a glass of water, or changing your shoes, before you permit yourself to respond.

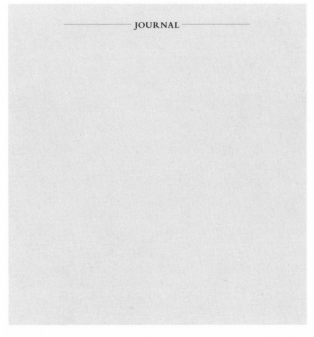

JOURNAL

CALMNESS

THE SAGE SAID TO HIS SON, "Do not envy your brother for what he has, for his life will remain pleasant but yours will be full of worry and grief." The sage said further, "The one who envies and the one who desires were created for nothing but anger."

—*ORCHOT TZADDIKIM* (1540)

PHRASE *Still waters of the heart.*

PRACTICE Set yourself an activity that you must do when you feel anger coming on, such as drinking a glass of water, or changing your shoes, before you permit yourself to respond.

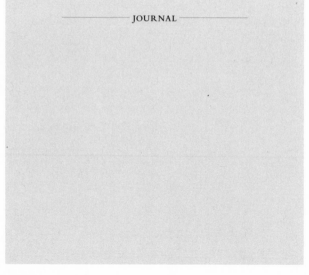

JOURNAL

THE RABBIS TAUGHT: Those who are insulted but do not insult, who hear their embarrassment but do not respond, they act with love and rejoice in their troubles, the Scripture says about them: "And God's beloved are like the sunrise in all its glory" (Judges 5:21).

—TALMUD, SHABBAT 88B

PHRASE   *Still waters of the heart.*

PRACTICE   Set yourself an activity that you must do when you feel anger coming on, such as drinking a glass of water, or changing your shoes, before you permit yourself to respond.

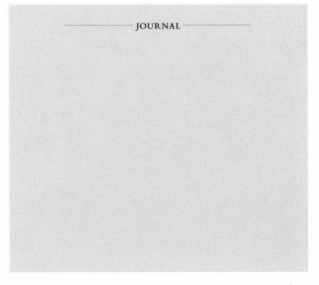

JOURNAL

RABBI SIMCHA ZISSEL ZIV of Kelm (1824–1898) developed a strategy to never to lose his temper. He had a special jacket that he had set aside to wear when he was angry. He said, "When I feel anger coming on, I know that I have to get my special jacket. But, by the time I do, I am no longer angry."

PHRASE *Still waters of the heart.*

PRACTICE Set yourself an activity that you must do when you feel anger coming on, such as drinking a glass of water, or changing your shoes, before you permit yourself to respond.

JOURNAL

THE WORDS OF THE WISE spoken in quiet are more acceptable than the cry of a ruler among fools.

—ECCLESIASTES 9:17

PHRASE   *Still waters of the heart.*

PRACTICE   Set yourself an activity that you must do when you feel anger coming on, such as drinking a glass of water, or changing your shoes, before you permit yourself to respond.

JOURNAL

PATIENCE

THE HEBREW TERM for patience is *savlanut*. It shares a linguistic root with *sevel,* which means "suffering," and *sabal,* which means "a porter." What could these three words possibly share in common? The answer is that being patient means bearing the burden of your own suffering. You tell yourself, I can bear these feelings on my inner shoulders. Holding them aloft and not crumpling under their weight, you are patient.

> The patient person shows much good sense, but the quick-tempered one displays folly at its height.
>
> —PROVERBS 14:29

PHRASE *Every person has their hour, everything its place.*

PRACTICE Identify the most likely situation to try your patience, and commit to "bearing the burden of your emotions" for at least five minutes in that situation.

JOURNAL

WHAT IS PATIENCE? The patient person is exactly like someone who is carrying a heavy package. Even though it weighs upon him, he continues to go on his way, and doesn't take a break from carrying it. The same is true in all the relationships that are between people: we see and hear many things that aren't according to our will, and still we continue to be good friends.

—RABBI SHLOMO WOLBE (1914–2005)

PHRASE *Every person has their hour, everything its place.*

PRACTICE Identify the most likely situation to try your patience, and commit to "bearing the burden of your emotions" for at least five minutes in that situation.

JOURNAL

RABBI PREIDA HAD a student whom he would teach each idea four hundred times, and then the student would learn it. One day the student was distracted and did not learn. Rabbi Preida said to him, "Pay attention and I will teach you," and he taught him the same lesson another four hundred times.

—TALMUD, ERUVIN 54B

PHRASE *Every person has their hour, everything its place.*

PRACTICE Identify the most likely situation to try your patience, and commit to "bearing the burden of your emotions" for at least five minutes in that situation.

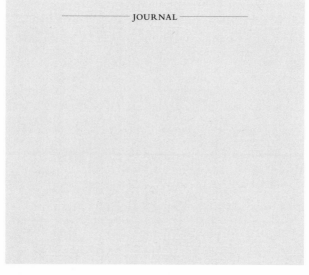

JOURNAL

YOU CAN TRAIN YOURSELF to be patient. You can train yourself to open the space between the match and the fuse.

—RABBI YECHIEL YITZCHOK PERR (B. 1935)

PHRASE *Every person has their hour, everything its place.*

PRACTICE Identify the most likely situation to try your patience, and commit to "bearing the burden of your emotions" for at least five minutes in that situation.

JOURNAL

WHAT IS THE GREATEST virtue? Patience with others' vices.

—RABBI SHLOMO IBN GABIROL (C. 1021–1058)

PHRASE *Every person has their hour, everything its place.*

PRACTICE Identify the most likely situation to try your patience, and commit to "bearing the burden of your emotions" for at least five minutes in that situation.

———— JOURNAL ————

How MUCH PATIENCE must a community leader have for the community? The same as a parent for a suckling child.

—TALMUD, SANHEDRIN 7A

PHRASE *Every person has their hour, everything its place.*

PRACTICE Identify the most likely situation to try your patience, and commit to "bearing the burden of your emotions" for at least five minutes in that situation.

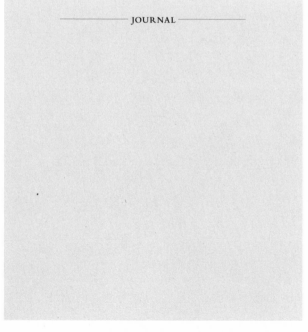

JOURNAL

PATIENCE

A PERSON SHOULD BE patient with one who has sinned
against him until his friend mends his ways, or until the
sin disappears of its own accord.

—RABBI MOSHE CORDOVERO (1522–1570)

PHRASE *Every person has their hour, everything its place.*

PRACTICE   Identify the most likely situation to try your
patience, and commit to "bearing the burden of your
emotions" for at least five minutes in that situation.

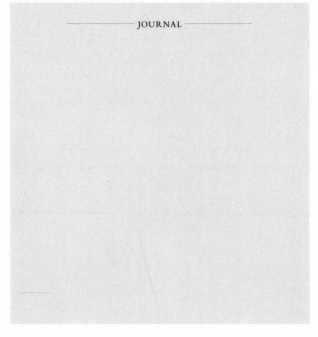

JOURNAL

LOVE

THE SINGLE, INTEGRATED inner experience of caring for, respecting, and bonding to another is love. The object of your love is one whom you care about even more than you are concerned for your own self. You would do or give what the other needs without the slightest feeling that what you have done or given is a sacrifice at all. Those acts and gifts are the fulfillment of love, and life.

> Rabbi Akiva taught: "'Love your neighbor as yourself' (Leviticus 19:18). This is the greatest principle of the Torah."
>
> —SIFRA, KEDOSHIM 2

PHRASE *Love the One and love His works.*

PRACTICE Seek opportunities to give gifts to those whom you want to love more—gifts of money, objects, time, caring, attention, and the like.

JOURNAL

LOVE

WHEN YOU LOVE SOMEONE, don't love him according to your preferences and desires, but according to his preferences and desires.

—RABBEINU YONAH OF GERONDI (D. 1263)

PHRASE *Love the One and love His works.*

PRACTICE Seek opportunities to give gifts to those whom you want to love more—gifts of money, objects, time, caring, attention, and the like.

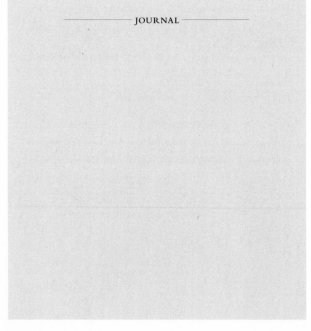

JOURNAL

WHEN TWO PEOPLE LOVE one another, they can stand together on the head of a pin. When two people hate one another, the whole world is not wide enough for them to coexist.

— RABBI SHLOMO IBN GABIROL (1021–1058)

PHRASE *Love the One and love His works.*

PRACTICE Seek opportunities to give gifts to those whom you want to love more—gifts of money, objects, time, caring, attention, and the like.

JOURNAL

LOVE

THE PATH TO ACQUIRING love of every person is to help each person with your soul and your money according to your ability. Helping with one's soul means serving all people, whether they are rich or poor, and trying on their behalf. Helping with one's money means lending to the wealthy when he needs money, and similarly the poor.

—*ORCHOT TZADDIKIM* (1540)

PHRASE *Love the One and love His works.*

PRACTICE Seek opportunities to give gifts to those whom you want to love more—gifts of money, objects, time, caring, attention, and the like.

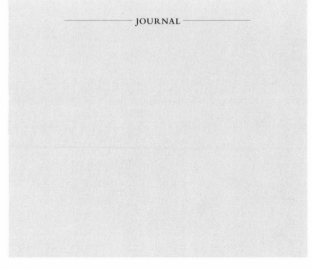

JOURNAL

LOVE OF ALL CREATURES is also love of God, for who- ever loves the One loves all the works that He has made. When one loves God, it is impossible not to love His creatures. The opposite is also true: If one hates the crea- tures, it is impossible to love God Who created them.

—RABBI YEHUDAH LOEW,
MAHARAL OF PRAGUE (1525–1609)

PHRASE   *Love the One and love His works.*

PRACTICE   Seek opportunities to give gifts to those whom you want to love more—gifts of money, ob- jects, time, caring, attention, and the like.

———— JOURNAL ————

LOVE

LOVE IS A CONSEQUENCE of giving. When a person gives, it is as if he is giving part of himself. He therefore loves the recipient because he finds in him something of himself. If his giving assumes great proportions and he lavishes loving-kindness on his neighbor with abundance, he will find himself included entirely in the other. Then he can love his neighbor as himself—completely as himself—without any distinction.

—RABBI ELIYAHU DESSLER (1892–1953)

PHRASE *Love the One and love His works.*

PRACTICE Seek opportunities to give gifts to those whom you want to love more—gifts of money, objects, time, caring, attention, and the like.

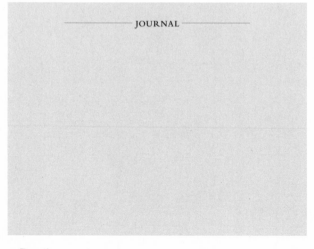

JOURNAL

IF YOU LOVE BUT YOU have not tasted the throes of jealousy, your love is not real love; for jealousy—the demand for exclusivity—completes love.

—RABBI ELIYAHU DE VIDAS (1518–1592)

PHRASE *Love the One and love His works.*

PRACTICE Seek opportunities to give gifts to those whom you want to love more—gifts of money, objects, time, caring, attention, and the like.

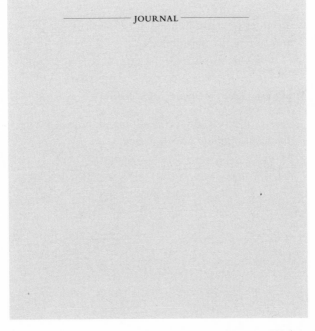

JOURNAL

ABSTINENCE

THOUGH JEWISH TRADITION does not stress abstinence as a spiritual practice, it recognizes that anyone who would climb a holy mountain must be able to draw a line and not cross it. The Mussar teachers affirm that our world is given to us to enjoy, but that we must also be the masters over our own gratifications. Only when we are capable of pushing away whatever calls to us can we say that our free will is truly intact.

> In order to attain holiness, it is essential for a person to practice abstinence.
> —RABBI MOSHE CHAIM LUZZATTO (1707–1746)

PHRASE *Learn to say no and be holy.*

PRACTICE Every day, say no to one thing you are in the habit of doing or consuming.

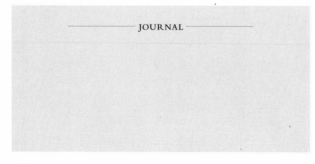

JOURNAL

WHEN THE EVIL INCLINATION overwhelms your reason and entices you, it steers you toward excess, which brings you to ruin and destroys your body. You need to abstain from the things that please and relax you to maintain balance.

—RABBI BAHYA IBN PAQUDA (11TH CENTURY)

PHRASE *Learn to say no and be holy.*

PRACTICE Every day, say no to one thing you are in the habit of doing or consuming.

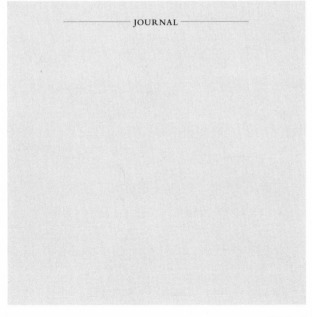

JOURNAL

RABBI AKIVA SAID: "Vows are a fence for abstinence" (Pirkei Avot 3:13). One who is firmly in control of himself and can achieve separation from worldly desires without making vows, should not make them. But if you see that your evil inclination is too strong for you, you should certainly erect many personal fences, in keeping with your temptations. Once you have succeeded in overcoming your desires, return to the path of moderation.

—RABBEINU YONAH OF GERONDI (D. 1263)

PHRASE *Learn to say no and be holy.*

PRACTICE Every day, say no to one thing you are in the habit of doing or consuming.

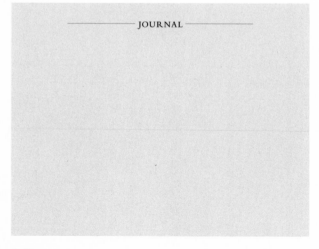

JOURNAL

A PERSON SHOULD SEPARATE himself from anything that is not essential to him in relation to the affairs of the world; if he separates himself from anything that is essential to him, regardless of the reason for its being so, he is a sinner. This principle is a consistent one. Its application to particular instances, however, is a matter of individual judgment.

—RABBI MOSHE CHAIM LUZZATTO (1707–1746)

PHRASE *Learn to say no and be holy.*

PRACTICE Every day, say no to one thing you are in the habit of doing or consuming.

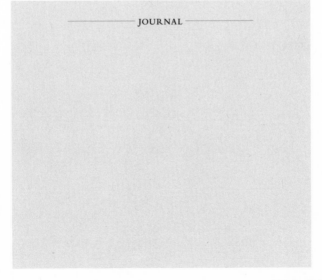

JOURNAL

ABSTINENCE

EAT ONLY ENOUGH TO SATISFY your hunger and you will protect yourself from trouble and preserve your health. Do not keep eating as long as the food still appeals to you, because the palate always wants more until the stomach is loaded. Eating like this will lead to all sorts of damage and disease.

—RABBEINU YONAH OF GERONDI (D. 1263)

PHRASE *Learn to say no and be holy.*

PRACTICE Every day, say no to one thing you are in the habit of doing or consuming.

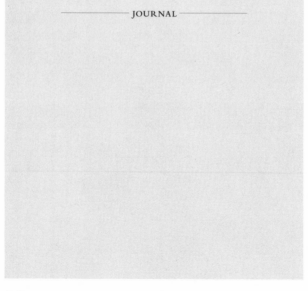

JOURNAL

ONE WHOSE HEART RENOUNCES the love of this world is truly abstinent, but one who yearns for its possessions, whose heart clings to them with love and grieves over their absence, is not truly abstinent.

—RABBI AVRAHAM BEN HARAMBAM (1186–1237)

PHRASE *Learn to say no and be holy.*

PRACTICE Every day, say no to one thing you are in the habit of doing or consuming.

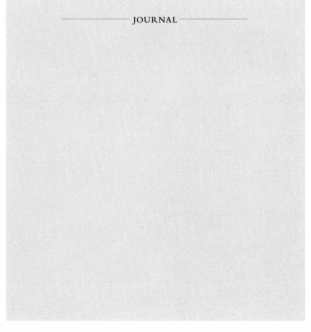

JOURNAL

ABSTINENCE

ABSTAIN EVEN FROM THINGS that are permitted, to avoid permitting yourself things that are forbidden.

—RABBI ELIEZER PAPO (1785–1826)

PHRASE   *Learn to say no and be holy.*

PRACTICE   Every day, say no to one thing you are in the habit of doing or consuming.

JOURNAL

COMPASSION

———

THE HEBREW TERM for compassion is related to the word that means "womb." When we perceive another person as being as intimately related to us as a fetus to its mother, how could we do anything but care about them? The trait of compassion can be understood as a benevolent feeling or sustaining action that follows from a perspective of intimate connection. Clean up and improve a relationship, and compassion will flow as a natural consequence.

> When a child's toy breaks, he feels as bad as an adult would feel if his factory were destroyed.
> —RABBI YISRAEL SALANTER (1810–1883)

PHRASE *Care for the other—we are one.*

PRACTICE Identify a person or people with whom there is heaviness in your relationship, then act toward them in a way that reaches beyond what is required, in order to relieve them of their burden.

——————— JOURNAL ———————

IN EVERYONE THERE IS ACTUALLY a part of his fellow man, and therefore a person should want his fellow's happiness and honor as much as his own, because he really is himself, and that is why we were commanded "love your neighbor as yourself."

—RABBI MOSHE CORDOVERO (1522–1570)

PHRASE *Care for the other—we are one.*

PRACTICE Identify a person or people with whom there is heaviness in your relationship, then act toward them in a way that reaches beyond what is required, in order to relieve them of their burden.

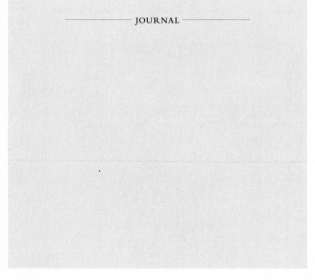

JOURNAL

IF ONE OF YOUR countrymen becomes poor and is unable to support himself among you, help him as you would an alien or a temporary resident, so he can continue to live among you.

—LEVITICUS 25:35

PHRASE   *Care for the other—we are one.*

PRACTICE   Identify a person or people with whom there is heaviness in your relationship, then act toward them in a way that reaches beyond what is required, in order to relieve them of their burden.

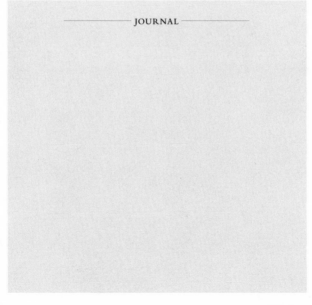

JOURNAL

COMPASSION

"MOSES GREW UP and went out to his brethren and saw their suffering" (Exodus 2:11). Even when he dwelled in Pharoah's palace, Moses was able to contemplate his brothers' pain, but he had to go out to them in order to see with his senses how they were suffering.

—RABBI SHLOMO WOLBE (1914–2005)

PHRASE *Care for the other—we are one.*

PRACTICE Identify a person or people with whom there is heaviness in your relationship, then act toward them in a way that reaches beyond what is required, in order to relieve them of their burden.

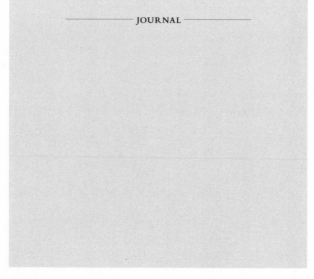

JOURNAL

"WHOEVER HAS COMPASSION on people, they will have mercy on him in Heaven" (Talmud, Shabbat 151b). This means that showing compassion for a fellow human being arouses the reservoirs of Heavenly Mercy, which catalyzes God to sit on the Throne of Compassion, rather than on the Throne of Strict Justice.

—RABBI ELIYAHU SCHLESSINGER (B. 1949)

PHRASE *Care for the other—we are one.*

PRACTICE Identify a person or people with whom there is heaviness in your relationship, then act toward them in a way that reaches beyond what is required, in order to relieve them of their burden.

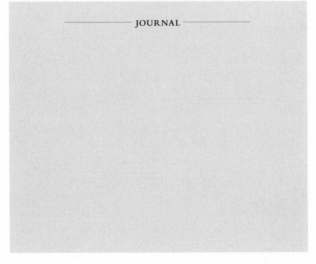

——————— JOURNAL ———————

COMPASSION

RABBI SHIMON the son of Elazar would say: "Do not appease your friend at the height of his anger; do not comfort him while his dead still lies before him; do not ask him about his vow the moment he makes it; and do not try to see him at the time of his degradation."

—PIRKEI AVOT 4:18

PHRASE *Care for the other—we are one.*

PRACTICE Identify a person or people with whom there is heaviness in your relationship, then act toward them in a way that reaches beyond what is required, in order to relieve them of their burden.

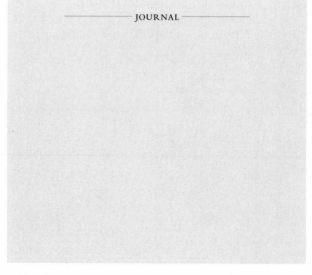

JOURNAL

A PIOUS JEW is not one who worries about his neighbor's soul and his own stomach; a pious Jew worries about his own soul and his neighbor's stomach.

—RABBI YISRAEL SALANTER (1810–1883)

PHRASE *Care for the other—we are one.*

PRACTICE Identify a person or people with whom there is heaviness in your relationship, then act toward them in a way that reaches beyond what is required, in order to relieve them of their burden.

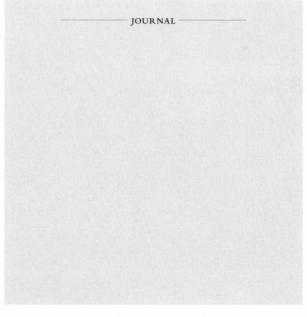

JOURNAL

MODESTY

THE CENTRAL CONCERN for modesty is to reserve for yourself a private world. Deeper still is the priority the Mussar teachers place on human dignity. Every human being is worthy of dignity beyond measure, simply by virtue of being made in the image and likeness of God. What can we do to preserve this inherent dignity? We can build a holy of holies in our own lives that does not put on public display that which is debased, rather than enhanced, by being flaunted before others.

> The dignity of the daughter of the king is inwardness.
>
> —PSALMS 45:14

PHRASE   *Wise privacy bestows dignity.*

PRACTICE   Whatever you might be tempted to flaunt, whether body, ideas, wealth, or any other gift, keep it hidden.

JOURNAL

ADAM AND EVE DID NOT know the way of modesty, nor have the ability to discriminate between good and evil, until they ate from the Tree of Knowledge. As it says, "and the eyes of both of them were opened" (Genesis 3:7).

—*ORCHOT TZADDIKIM* (1540)

PHRASE *Wise privacy bestows dignity.*

PRACTICE Whatever you might be tempted to flaunt, whether body, ideas, wealth, or any other gift, keep it hidden.

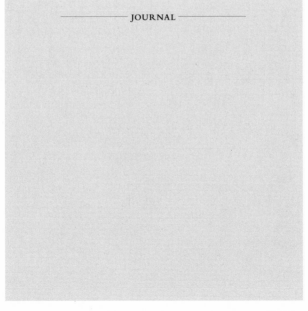

JOURNAL

MODESTY

DISTANCE YOURSELF FROM all that is ugly and un-
seemly, from lust and from anything that will lead people
to be suspicious of you, and you will find favor in the
eyes of God and man.

—RABBI MENACHEM MENDEL LEFFIN (1749–1826)

PHRASE   *Wise privacy bestows dignity.*

PRACTICE   Whatever you might be tempted to flaunt,
whether body, ideas, wealth, or any other gift, keep it
hidden.

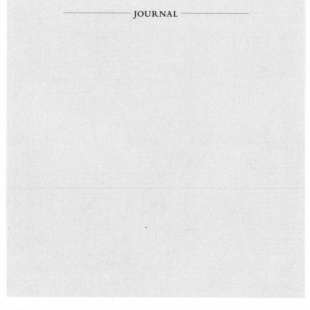

JOURNAL

MODESTY IS NOT ABOUT being covered up, but about awareness of a private life and of personal dignity. Today this concept of private dignity does not exist. As a result, everything is flaunted, everything is public.

—RABBI YAAKOV WEINBERG (1923–1999)

PHRASE   *Wise privacy bestows dignity.*

PRACTICE   Whatever you might be tempted to flaunt, whether body, ideas, wealth, or any other gift, keep it hidden.

JOURNAL

MODESTY

Rabbi Yochanan said: "Had the Torah not been given, we would learn modesty from the cat," which defecates in private and hides its waste.

—TALMUD, ERUVIN 100B

PHRASE *Wise privacy bestows dignity.*

PRACTICE Whatever you might be tempted to flaunt, whether body, ideas, wealth, or any other gift, keep it hidden.

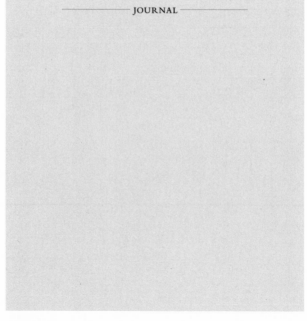

JOURNAL

A YOUNG STUDENT asked permission to go to a wedding. Rabbi Eliyahu Lopian (1872–1970) asked him if there might be women there dressed immodestly. The student replied that he had prepared a strategy: he wouldn't look. Rabbi Lopian turned to the student and said, "I'm already over eighty years old, and blind in one eye, yet despite this, I look!"

PHRASE   *Wise privacy bestows dignity.*

PRACTICE   Whatever you might be tempted to flaunt, whether body, ideas, wealth, or any other gift, keep it hidden.

--------------------- JOURNAL ---------------------

Week 18, Day 6

MODESTY

WHEN PRIDE COMES, so comes shame; but the modest ones will achieve wisdom.

—PROVERBS 11:2

PHRASE   *Wise privacy bestows dignity.*

PRACTICE   Whatever you might be tempted to flaunt, whether body, ideas, wealth, or any other gift, keep it hidden.

———— JOURNAL ————

WILLINGNESS

―――

WHEN CONFRONTED BY an opportunity, or a trying situation, all sorts of reasons can arise that steer us away from active engagement. Imagine coming to the end of your life and realizing how much you missed because you leaned away from life instead of gently and wisely leaning into the challenges and possibilities. Willingness means being ready to engage, contribute, and even risk. When the children of Israel came to the Red Sea, it only split for them once Nachshon ben Aminadav walked into the water up to his chin.

> We will do and we will hear.
>
> ―EXODUS 24:7

PHRASE   *The whole heart steps forward.*

PRACTICE   As much as possible, when you feel the impulse to answer a request with "no," say "yes."

――――――――― JOURNAL ―――――――――

WILLINGNESS

THE VIRTUE AND BENEFIT of willingness are seen in their relationship to life, as they are the fount of good and the source of loving-kindness.

—*ORCHOT TZADDIKIM* (1540)

PHRASE   *The whole heart steps forward.*

PRACTICE   As much as possible, when you feel the impulse to answer a request with "no," say "yes."

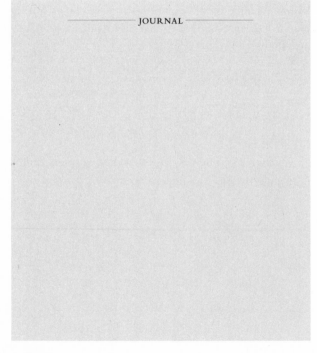

JOURNAL

WHEN IT IS NECESSARY to send a letter, I send a telegram; when it is necessary to send a telegram, I send an emissary; when it is necessary to send an emissary, I go myself.

—RABBI YOSEF YOZEL HURWITZ,
THE ALTER OF NOVARDOK (1849–1919)

PHRASE *The whole heart steps forward.*

PRACTICE As much as possible, when you feel the impulse to answer a request with "no," say "yes."

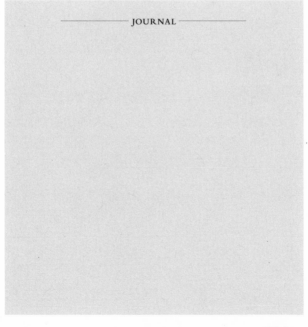

——————— JOURNAL ———————

WILLINGNESS

IF YOU ARE WILLING, and listen, then you will eat the good of the land.

—PROVERBS 8:34

PHRASE *The whole heart steps forward.*

PRACTICE As much as possible, when you feel the impulse to answer a request with "no," say "yes."

——— JOURNAL ———

IN TIMES SUCH AS OURS, when capable people are scarce, anyone who shows willingness to tackle a vital problem has divine assistance heaped upon him.

—RABBI ELIYAHU DESSLER (1892–1953)

PHRASE *The whole heart steps forward.*

PRACTICE As much as possible, when you feel the impulse to answer a request with "no," say "yes."

JOURNAL

WILLINGNESS

"THE ONE WHO answers 'amen' is greater than the one who makes the blessing" (Talmud, Nazir 66b). Why? Because this indicates willingness to accept the obligation of the words.

—RABBI SIMCHA ZISSEL ZIV,
THE ALTER OF KELM (1824–1898)

PHRASE *The whole heart steps forward.*

PRACTICE As much as possible, when you feel the impulse to answer a request with "no," say "yes."

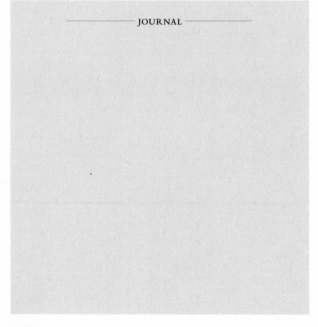

JOURNAL

I KNOW, MY GOD, that You test the heart and are pleased with integrity. All these things I have given willingly and with honest intent. And now I have seen with joy how willingly Your people who are here have given to You.

—I CHRONICLES 29:16–18

PHRASE *The whole heart steps forward.*

PRACTICE As much as possible, when you feel the impulse to answer a request with "no," say "yes."

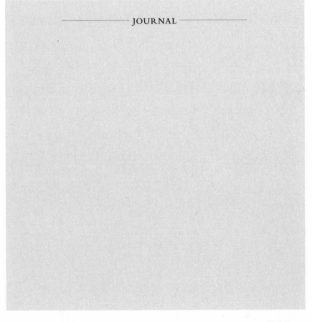

JOURNAL

SIMPLICITY

THE HEBREW *histapkut* can be translated as "simplicity," "frugality," or "contentment." Each translation picks up on a different facet of this inner attitude. The Mussar teachings encourage us to live a more simple and spiritual life. But they go one step further: don't live simply while regretting and resenting all you have given up. And to go one step further still: the heart is freed to pursue holiness when you *rejoice* in what you have.

> Ben Zoma said: Who is rich? One who is happy with his lot.
>
> —PIRKEI AVOT 4:1

PHRASE *Rejoice in my portion.*

PRACTICE Reduce your consumption in a different area of your life every day.

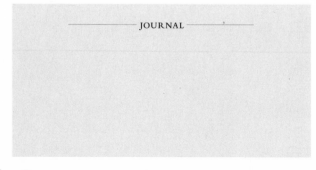

———— JOURNAL ————

WHO SEEKS MORE than he needs, hinders himself from enjoying what he has. Seek what you need and give up what you need not. For in giving up what you don't need, you'll learn what you really do need.

—RABBI SHLOMO IBN GABIROL (1021–1058)

PHRASE   *Rejoice in my portion.*

PRACTICE   Reduce your consumption in a different area of your life every day.

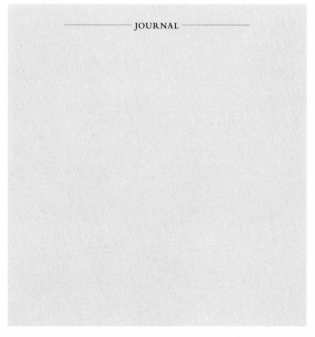

JOURNAL

SIMPLICITY

HUMAN BEINGS AVIDLY pursue worldly pleasures because they have a subconscious urge to still the pangs of spiritual hunger. Everyone has this nameless inner yearning: the longing of the soul for its state of perfection. And indulgence in worldly pleasures is an illusory substitute for this.

—RABBI ELIYAHU DESSLER (1892–1953)

PHRASE *Rejoice in my portion.*

PRACTICE Reduce your consumption in a different area of your life every day.

JOURNAL

THE LUXURIES WE indulge in eventually come to seem to be necessities, as if we could not live without them.

—RABBI YISRAEL SALANTER (1810–1883)

PHRASE *Rejoice in my portion.*

PRACTICE Reduce your consumption in a different area of your life every day.

——— JOURNAL ———

SIMPLICITY

To BE CONTENT means to be satisfied with the material possessions one has. One who wants more than he has is suffering from "desire." All transgressions stem from desire. Its opposite—contentment—is the basis for the whole Torah.

—THE VILNA GAON (1720–1797)

PHRASE   *Rejoice in my portion.*

PRACTICE   Reduce your consumption in a different area of your life every day.

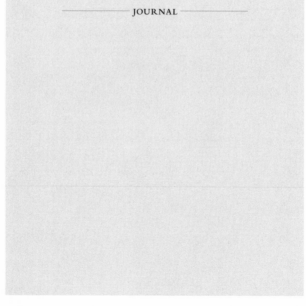

JOURNAL

LIVING LAVISHLY, we then make our bellies our gods, our clothing our Torah, and the condition of our fine homes our morals. In our errors we plunge to the depths of foolishness and become content with laziness and laden with desires.

—RABBI BAHYA IBN PAQUDA (11TH CENTURY)

PHRASE *Rejoice in my portion.*

PRACTICE Reduce your consumption in a different area of your life every day.

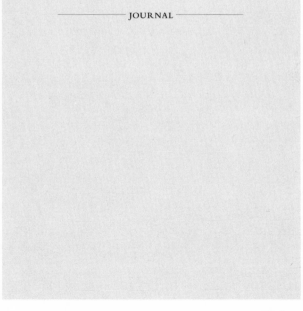

JOURNAL

SIMPLICITY

IVORY PALACES built on earth
   and mansions lined with galleries
with marble columns on inlaid floors
   in spacious halls that filled with parties:
in a flash I saw them all as rubble
   and weathered ruins without a soul.

—MOSHE IBN EZRA (C. 1055–C. 1138)

PHRASE *Rejoice in my portion.*

PRACTICE Reduce your consumption in a different
area of your life every day.

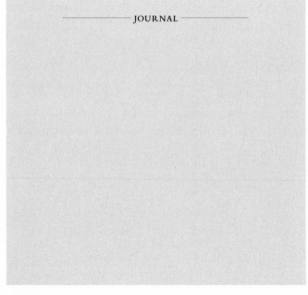

JOURNAL

COURAGE

In Jewish thought, the heart is not just the emotional center, it is the kaleidoscopic core of our inner being. Among its many qualities, the heart can be strong or weak, and the strong heart—*ametz lev* in Hebrew—is what gives rise to courage. The strong heart boldly pursues what is right and what is called for, without succumbing to anxiety or fear about its own safety or benefit.

Be strong and of good courage.

—JOSHUA 1:9

PHRASE *Forward and upward, strong heart.*

PRACTICE Undertake the thing you could have done or should have done, and now will do, through strength of heart.

JOURNAL

COURAGE

AT TIMES OF DISTRESS, strengthen your heart,
  Even if you stand at death's door.
  The lamp has light before it is extinguished.
  Wounded lions still know how to roar.

—SHMUEL HA'NAGGID (993–C. 1056)

PHRASE *Forward and upward, strong heart.*

PRACTICE Undertake the thing you could have done or should have done, and now will do, through strength of heart.

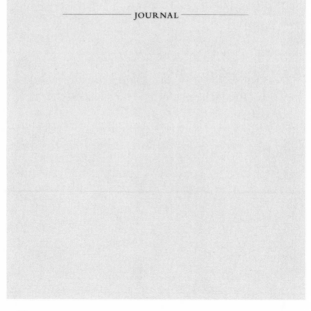

JOURNAL

IN 1918, BOLSHEVIK SOLDIERS burst into the No-vardok yeshiva. The commanding officer marched straight to the head of the yeshiva, pulled his gun, and demanded that the yeshiva be closed immediately. The young man rose from his seat, unbuttoned his shirt, and said, "Shoot!" The younger students lined up behind him, unbuttoned their shirts, and waited. The soldiers turned and left.

PHRASE   *Forward and upward, strong heart.*

PRACTICE   Undertake the thing you could have done or should have done, and now will do, through strength of heart.

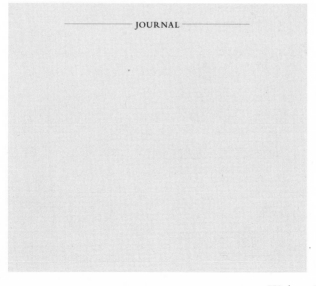

JOURNAL

COURAGE

EVERY SIN CAUSES a special anxiety on the spirit, which can only be erased by repentance, which transforms the anxiety itself into inner security and courage.

—RABBI ABRAHAM ISAAC KOOK (1865–1935)

PHRASE *Forward and upward, strong heart.*

PRACTICE Undertake the thing you could have done or should have done, and now will do, through strength of heart.

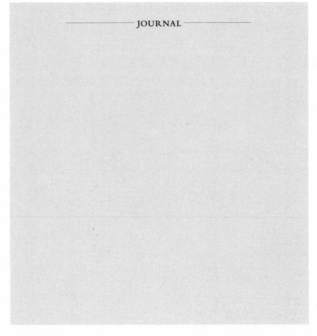

JOURNAL

ONLY HE WHO HAS the courage to face up to his own wrongdoing and determines to change his ways will find divine mercy.

—RABBI SOLOMON BREUER (1850–1926)

PHRASE *Forward and upward, strong heart.*

PRACTICE Undertake the thing you could have done or should have done, and now will do, through strength of heart.

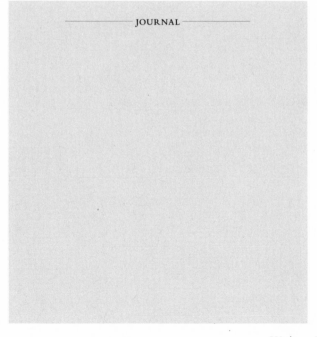

JOURNAL

COURAGE

LET THE GOD-FEARING people take courage and conquer evil. What can stop them?

—RABBI YISRAEL SALANTER (1810–1883)

PHRASE *Forward and upward, strong heart.*

PRACTICE Undertake the thing you could have done or should have done, and now will do, through strength of heart.

JOURNAL

JUDAH THE SON OF TEIMA would say: be bold as a leopard, light as an eagle, swift as a deer, and mighty as a lion to do the will of your Father in Heaven.

—PIRKEI AVOT 5:20

PHRASE *Forward and upward, strong heart.*

PRACTICE Undertake the thing you could have done or should have done, and now will do, through strength of heart.

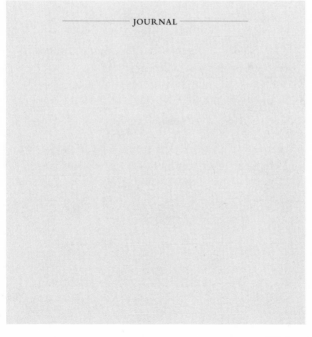

———— JOURNAL ————

Week 21, Day 7

TRUST

WHILE HUMILITY DEFINES our sense of self, the trait of trust defines how we are in relationships. Whom we trust reveals who or what we rely on in life. Can we rely on ourselves, knowing our own limitations and frailties? Can we fully trust others, knowing that people test us in our lives? Can we trust God? Here the answer is a resounding "yes," because only the One who created this entire dramatic universe is responsible for both the underlying script and stage directions of life.

> The essence of trust is the tranquility of the soul enjoyed by the one who trusts.
>
> —RABBI BAHYA IBN PAQUDA (11TH CENTURY)

PHRASE   *I rest in the hands of my Maker.*

PRACTICE   When you feel worried, recite the phrase, "My life is in the hands of the One who made me."

——— JOURNAL ———

BLESSED BE THE ONE who trusts in the Lord and the Lord shall be his source of trust. You shall be like a tree planted by waters, sending forth its roots by a stream; you will not sense the coming of heat, your leaves are ever fresh; you have no care in years of drought, you do not cease to yield fruit.

—JEREMIAH 17:7–8

PHRASE *I rest in the hands of my Maker.*

PRACTICE When you feel worried, recite the phrase, "My life is in the hands of the One who made me."

———— JOURNAL ————

TRUST

A PERSON WHO TRIES to practice trust in God while leaving himself a backup plan is like a person who tries to learn how to swim but insists on keeping one foot on the ground.

—RABBI YOSEF YOZEL HURWITZ,
THE ALTER OF NOVARDOK (1849–1919)

PHRASE   *I rest in the hands of my Maker.*

PRACTICE   When you feel worried, recite the phrase, "My life is in the hands of the One who made me."

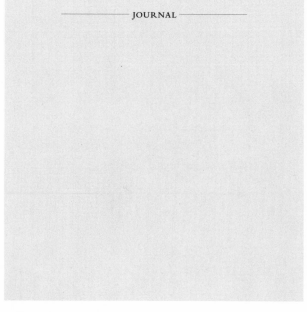

JOURNAL

THE MANNA TEACHES US to have trust in God. For the entire forty years that the Jewish people were in the desert, they lived completely on their trust in God. They wandered in the arid wasteland without food for to-morrow's meal. It was impossible to leave over some of the manna for the following day. This national experience brought the entire nation to a very high level of trust.

—RABBI CHAIM SHMULEVITZ (1902–1979)

PHRASE *I rest in the hands of my Maker.*

PRACTICE When you feel worried, recite the phrase, "My life is in the hands of the One who made me."

JOURNAL

IF WORRY COMES to your heart, take it as a warning from God who loves you. Examine your deeds and take counsel with those whose advice you seek. When you have fulfilled God's will, trust God and your serenity will return.

—RABBI MENACHEM MENDEL LEFFIN (1749–1826)

PHRASE *I rest in the hands of my Maker.*

PRACTICE When you feel worried, recite the phrase, "My life is in the hands of the One who made me."

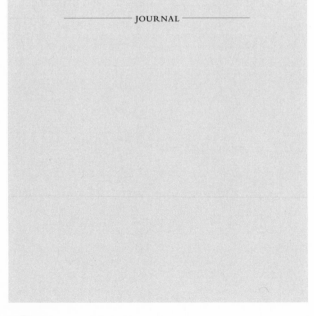

JOURNAL

THE GREATEST CHALLENGE a person faces is that he not be overwhelmed with the concerns of this world so that he forgets his purpose. Therefore, he should trust in God that He will supply his needs and sustain him, and that he will have time available to turn his heart to God.

—*ORCHOT TZADDIKIM* (1540)

PHRASE *I rest in the hands of my Maker.*

PRACTICE When you feel worried, recite the phrase, "My life is in the hands of the One who made me."

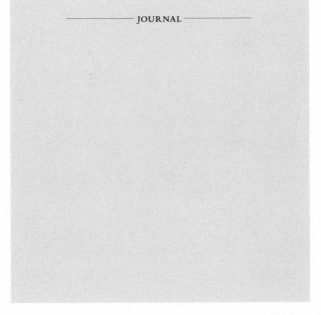

JOURNAL

TRUST

ONE WHO TRUSTS in God is surrounded by loving-kindness.

—PSALMS 32:10

PHRASE *I rest in the hands of my Maker.*

PRACTICE When you feel worried, recite the phrase, "My life is in the hands of the One who made me."

———— JOURNAL ————

FAITH

———

FAITH IN JEWISH thought is not a matter of belief, but rather a personal and immediate awareness of a single, benevolent, spiritual Creator of the universe. We refer to this source as HaShem, "the Name," signaling that we cannot hope to name the unnamable. In Mussar, faith is not so much something held as pursued. How could it be otherwise when relating to a divinity that is not only hidden, but that has hidden that very hiddenness?

The righteous shall live by his faith.

—HABAKKUK 2:4

PHRASE   *Cleave to the One and be whole.*

PRACTICE   Say the phrase "God willing" before undertaking any action, large or small.

——————— JOURNAL ———————

FAITH

IT IS IMPORTANT to visualize mentally the two paths that are before you. One path leads to the Garden of Eden, eternal bliss. The other path leads to tremendous suffering. When you see this clearly enough, you will have a strong inner feeling. This will become part of your reality and will have major ramifications in your way of life. Developing this awareness is a high priority. Do all you can to internalize faith and live with it daily.

—RABBI YISRAEL SALANTER (1810–1883)

PHRASE *Cleave to the One and be whole.*

PRACTICE Say the phrase "God willing" before undertaking any action, large or small.

——————— JOURNAL ———————

WHERE, LORD, will I find you:
your place is high and obscured.
   And where
      Won't I find you:
   your glory fills the world....
I sought your nearness:
with all my heart I called you.
   And in my going
      out to meet you,
   I found you coming toward me.
                    —YEHUDA HA'LEVI (C. 1075–1141)

PHRASE *Cleave to the One and be whole.*

PRACTICE Say the phrase "God willing" before undertaking any action, large or small.

——————— JOURNAL ———————

NOT WITH DEPRESSION, not with fearfulness, not with sentimental weakness must we turn to the divine light, but with a clear knowledge that what flows from the depths of our heart to approach God is a natural, complete, and healthy faculty. It is more than just a natural faculty—it is the basic, natural faculty of our soul.

—RABBI ABRAHAM ISAAC KOOK (1865–1935)

PHRASE   *Cleave to the One and be whole.*

PRACTICE   Say the phrase "God willing" before undertaking any action, large or small.

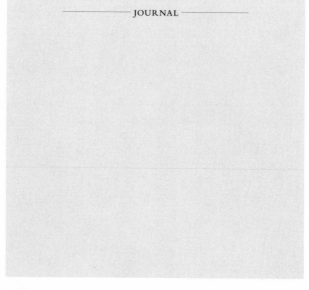

——— JOURNAL ———

THE TRUTH IS THAT there is no essential difference between the natural and the miraculous. Everything that occurs is a miracle. The world has no other cause but the will of God.

—RABBI ELIYAHU DESSLER (1892–1953)

PHRASE   *Cleave to the One and be whole.*

PRACTICE   Say the phrase "God willing" before undertaking any action, large or small.

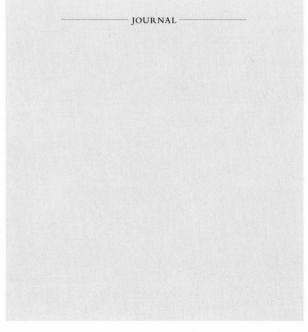

——————— JOURNAL ———————

FAITH

WE SEE THAT the sun shines upon the world, but we nevertheless praise God and say about Him in the morning prayers that "He illuminates the world and its inhabitants." Only, He does this via a conduit that is called the sun.

—RABBI CHAIM FRIEDLANDER (1923–1986)

PHRASE   *Cleave to the One and be whole.*

PRACTICE   Say the phrase "God willing" before undertaking any action, large or small.

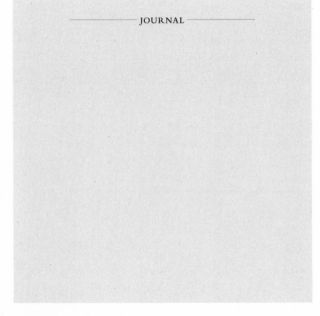

JOURNAL

THE BODY NEEDS AIR. What is the air of the soul? Faith.
—RABBI ELIYAHU LOPIAN (1872–1970)

PHRASE *Cleave to the One and be whole.*

PRACTICE Say the phrase "God willing" before undertaking any action, large or small.

JOURNAL

TRUTH

TRUTH IMPLIES KNOWLEDGE of things as they are, as they were, and as they will be. In that sense, the territory of truth is defined by connection to reality—past, present, and future. To know the truth and say something different is not necessarily wrong; the real issue of truth arises when you are thinking, speaking, and acting without awareness of reality. The Torah commands, "Be distant from falsehood," as a principle for living, because falsehood shakes the foundations of the world.

The signature of the Holy Blessed One is truth.

—TALMUD, SHABBAT 55A

PHRASE *Truth stands forever; falsehood has no legs.*

PRACTICE Check your words before you speak to ensure that they are true.

JOURNAL

EVEN AFTER THE DESIRES of one's heart have persuaded him to accept the false way as true, he still knows in his heart of hearts that the true path is "truer" than the other one. Every human being thus has the faculty of determining in his own heart where the real truth lies.

—RABBI ELIYAHU DESSLER (1892–1953)

PHRASE   *Truth stands forever; falsehood has no legs.*

PRACTICE   Check your words before you speak to ensure that they are true.

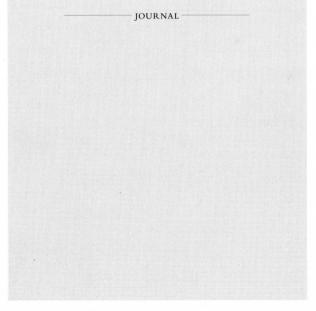

JOURNAL

TRUTH

IN THE END, falsehood has no base on which to stand. And if the liar should later speak truthfully, no one believes him any longer.

—RABBI MENACHEM MENDEL LEFFIN (1749–1826)

PHRASE *Truth stands forever; falsehood has no legs.*

PRACTICE Check your words before you speak to ensure that they are true.

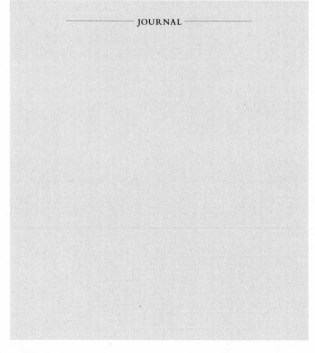

JOURNAL

DELAY YOUR speech
   if you want your words
to be straight and free of deceit—
as a master archer
   is slow to take aim
when splitting a grain of wheat.

      —SHMUEL HA'NAGGID (993–C. 1056)

PHRASE   *Truth stands forever; falsehood has no legs.*

PRACTICE   Check your words before you speak to ensure that they are true.

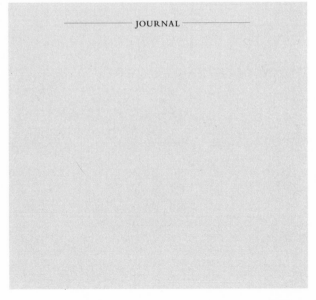

JOURNAL

TRUTH

LOVE TRUTH AND RIGHTEOUSNESS, and hew stead-
fastly to them, for the success you shall thereby attain
will be built upon a foundation of solid bedrock.

—RABBI MOSHE BEN MAIMON, THE RAMBAM (1135–1204)

PHRASE *Truth stands forever; falsehood has no legs.*

PRACTICE Check your words before you speak to
ensure that they are true.

——————— JOURNAL ———————

THE HEBREW WORD for "truth" is composed of the
three letters that are the first, middle, and last letters of
the Hebrew alphabet. The three Hebrew letters that spell
"falsehood" stand next to one another. This tells us that
truth creates a firm foundation, like the three legs of
a stool, while falsehood is unstable because it stands on a
narrow base.

PHRASE *Truth stands forever; falsehood has no legs.*

PRACTICE Check your words before you speak to
ensure that they are true.

JOURNAL

Week 24, Day 6

TRUTH

T̲ᴇᴀᴄʜ ʏᴏᴜʀ ᴛᴏɴɢᴜᴇ to say, "I do not know," lest you invent something and be trapped.

—ᴛᴀʟᴍᴜᴅ, ʙᴇʀᴀᴄʜᴏᴛ 4ᴀ

ᴘʜʀᴀsᴇ *Truth stands forever; falsehood has no legs.*

ᴘʀᴀᴄᴛɪᴄᴇ Check your words before you speak to ensure that they are true.

JOURNAL

SILENCE

———

SILENCE OF THE LIPS means not speaking. In contemplative silence, even the inner dialogue is stilled. The two are not related, each comprising its own virtue. The tongue is the pen of the heart, and the ability to be silent demonstrates a high level of self-mastery. To be inwardly still, however, is to abide in a suspended state of receptive reverence. It is prayer without words, a prayer prayed by the act of presence.

> Silence is becoming for the wise, how much more so, for fools!
>
> —TALMUD, PESACHIM 99B

PHRASE *Wisdom walks through the door of silence.*

PRACTICE Find at least ten minutes every day when you will be silent and seek inner stillness.

——— JOURNAL ———

SILENCE

ALL MY LIFE I have been raised among sages, and I have found nothing better for a person than silence.

—RABBAN SHIMON BEN GAMLIEL
(C. 10 B.C.E.–70 C.E.)

PHRASE *Wisdom walks through the door of silence.*

PRACTICE Find at least ten minutes every day when you will be silent and seek inner stillness.

JOURNAL

JUST AS THERE IS A TIME to open and a time to close the door of a house, so should one close the doors of his mouth. Just as you would guard silver, gold, and pearls in your room, within a case, making one enclosure within another, do the same with your mouth.

—*ORCHOT TZADDIKIM* (1540)

PHRASE   *Wisdom walks through the door of silence.*

PRACTICE   Find at least ten minutes every day when you will be silent and seek inner stillness.

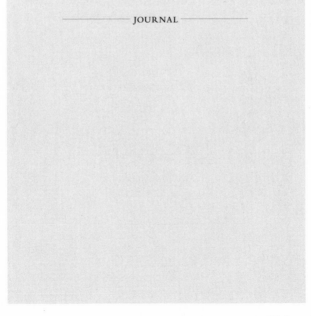

JOURNAL

SILENCE

THE CRAFT OF A PERSON in this world is to behave as if mute! The craft is not to be a babbler. This is something one has to learn: a baby knows how to talk and babbles as it pleases him. Silence needs to be learned, because silence is a great skill, and by it you recognize the person of intelligence. The nature of a person is his solitude. That's the only way for the soul and spirit to develop their strength.

—RABBI SHLOMO WOLBE (1914–2005)

PHRASE *Wisdom walks through the door of silence.*

PRACTICE Find at least ten minutes every day when you will be silent and seek inner stillness.

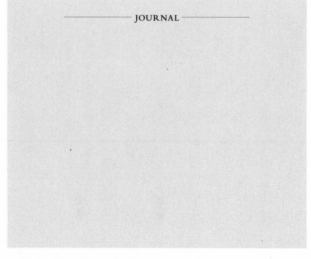

JOURNAL

THE LESS SAID, the fewer mistakes;
the greater the talk, the greater the headache.

—YOSEF QIMHI (C. 1160–1235)

PHRASE *Wisdom walks through the door of silence.*

PRACTICE Find at least ten minutes every day when you will be silent and seek inner stillness.

JOURNAL

SILENCE

SOME SILENCE MEANS cessation of speech. Another silence means cessation of thought. That silence arrives
together with the most hidden, beautiful, and exalted
thought.

—RABBI ABRAHAM ISAAC KOOK (1865–1935)

PHRASE *Wisdom walks through the door of silence.*

PRACTICE Find at least ten minutes every day when
you will be silent and seek inner stillness.

JOURNAL

OUR SAGES SAID that observance of the commandments and teachings are not enough to counterbalance what comes out of a person's mouth. "What should be a person's pursuit in this world? He should be silent" (Talmud, Chullin 89a). One must seal his lips as tight as two millstones.

—THE VILNA GAON (1720–1797)

PHRASE *Wisdom walks through the door of silence.*

PRACTICE Find at least ten minutes every day when you will be silent and seek inner stillness.

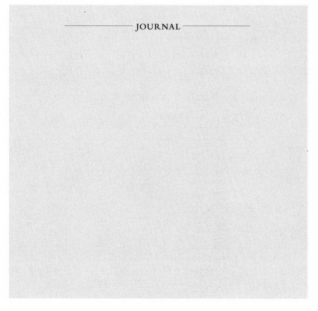

JOURNAL

AWE

———

AWE IS A human experience of the transcendent piercing apparent reality, a glimpse of the supreme within the mundane. However it may come to us, a moment of awe gives us a small taste of the cosmic mystery, and an intuitive intimation of the divine. Awe does not protest phenomenal reality; rather, it offers direct affirmation of the eternal that lies within the worldly. Awe is an invitation to seek, delivered directly to the heart.

> Praiseworthy is the person who is always filled with awe.
>
> —PROVERBS 28:14

PHRASE *The beginning of wisdom is awe.*

PRACTICE Put yourself in places that bring out the experience of awe in you.

——— JOURNAL ———

AWE

THERE ARE TWO TYPES of reverence of Heaven—the fear of future accountability and the awe of divine majesty. It must be stressed, however, that the two are not equal. It is clear that the awe of God's majesty is on a more exalted plane than the fear of future accountability.

—RABBI YITZCHAK BLAZER (1840–1907)

PHRASE   *The beginning of wisdom is awe.*

PRACTICE   Put yourself in places that bring out the experience of awe in you.

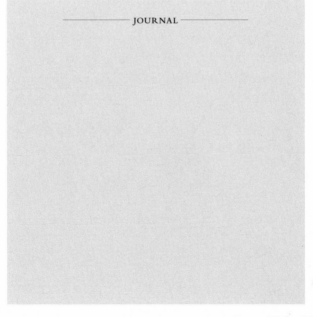

JOURNAL

AWE

To WHAT MAY Awe be likened? To the tremor of fear that a father feels when his beloved young son rides his shoulders as he dances with him and rejoices before him, taking care that he not fall off. Here there is joy that is incomparable, pleasure that is incomparable. And the fear tied up with them is pleasant, too. It does not impede the freedom of dance.

—RABBI AVRAHAM ELYA KAPLAN (1890–1924)

PHRASE *The beginning of wisdom is awe.*

PRACTICE Put yourself in places that bring out the experience of awe in you.

——— JOURNAL ———

IT IS THE DUTY of conscientious people to constantly reflect that God's glory fills the whole world: we are ever in His presence and must fulfill His will. This is the meaning of the verse: "I set HaShem before me always" (Psalms 16:8).

—RABBI ISRAEL MEIR KAGAN,
THE CHOFETZ CHAIM (1838–1933)

PHRASE *The beginning of wisdom is awe.*

PRACTICE Put yourself in places that bring out the experience of awe in you.

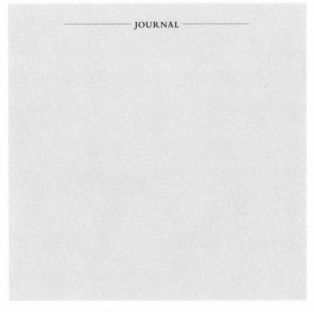

JOURNAL

AWE

Man's only hope is to fortify himself with the reverence of the Almighty. This reverence is an impregnable fortress that can deliver him from every enemy and attack. It is mighty enough to bind his desires and prevent the evil intentions of his heart from bursting into a destructive behavior.

—RABBI YITZCHAK BLAZER (1840–1907)

PHRASE *The beginning of wisdom is awe.*

PRACTICE Put yourself in places that bring out the experience of awe in you.

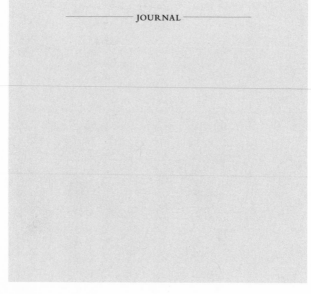

JOURNAL

ONCE IT HAS BECOME clear to one that wherever he may be, he is standing before the presence of the Holy One, there will come to him of itself, the awe and fear of going astray in his actions so that they do not accord with the majesty of the Blessed One.

—RABBI MOSHE CHAIM LUZZATTO (1707–1746)

PHRASE *The beginning of wisdom is awe.*

PRACTICE Put yourself in places that bring out the experience of awe in you.

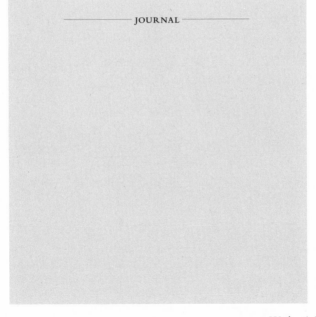

JOURNAL

AWE

OF ALL THE WAYS of awakening inner reverence in man, the best is the contemplation of the works of God. Their transcendent greatness must inspire awe.

—RABBI ELIYAHU DE VIDAS (1518–1592)

PHRASE *The beginning of wisdom is awe.*

PRACTICE Put yourself in places that bring out the experience of awe in you.

———— JOURNAL ————

Week 26, Day 7

GRATITUDE

GRATITUDE BEGINS with recognizing the good that comes your way—something most of us don't do naturally. Once that good is seen and named, the next step is to acknowledge it as a gift, not something you deserve. And all gifts merit an expression of thanks. Gratitude includes saying thank-you for the gift and to the source of the gift, be that God or a human being.

> It is good to give thanks to the Lord and to sing praises to Your name, O Most High; to proclaim Your goodness in the morning and Your faithfulness at night.
>
> —PSALMS 92:1–2

PHRASE *Awaken to the good and give thanks.*

PRACTICE Find something that is good in every situation, and acknowledge it as good.

———— JOURNAL ————

THE MUSSAR TEACHER Rabbi Eliyahu Lopian (1872–1970) was once talking to a student after prayers, and at the same time was folding up his *tallis* (prayer shawl). The *tallis* was large and he had to rest it on a bench to fold it. After he had finished the folding, Reb Elya noticed that the bench was dusty, and so he headed out to fetch a towel to wipe it off. The student to whom he was speaking ran to get the towel for him. Reb Elya held up his hand. "No! No! I must clean it myself, for I must show my gratitude to the bench upon which I folded my *tallis*."

PHRASE *Awaken to the good and give thanks.*

PRACTICE Find something that is good in every situation, and acknowledge it as good.

JOURNAL

WE ARE GRATEFUL TO YOU, for it is You our God, and God of our ancestors forever and ever, rock of our lives, shield of our salvation. You are the One from generation to generation. We will thank You and speak of Your praise—for our lives, which we have entrusted to Your hand, and for our souls, which You keep secure, and for Your miracles, which we encounter every day, and for Your perpetual wonders and favors—evening, and morning, and afternoon. You are goodness whose compassion never fails and You are the compassionate One whose loving-kindness knows no bounds. Ever will we place our hope in You.

—MODIM ANACHNU PRAYER,
FROM THE JEWISH PRAYER BOOK

PHRASE   *Awaken to the good and give thanks.*

PRACTICE   Find something that is good in every situation, and acknowledge it as good.

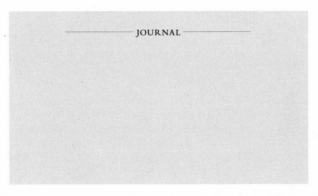

JOURNAL

HERE IS THE PRINCIPLE: the recipient's gratitude should not depend on the effort expended on his behalf. Deriving benefit from someone or something in and of itself requires an expression of gratitude. This appreciation must be shown not only to human beings, but to lower orders of creation as well.

—RABBI CHAIM SHMULEVITZ (1902–1979)

PHRASE *Awaken to the good and give thanks.*

PRACTICE Find something that is good in every situation, and acknowledge it as good.

————— JOURNAL —————

BEN ZOMA USED TO SAY: "A good guest says, 'How much my host worked for me! He put so much meat, wine, and bread in front of me—all his exertion was just for me!' A bad guest says, 'What did my host toil for me? I ate just one roll, just one piece of meat, I drank just one cup—all his exertion was for his own household!'"

—TALMUD, BERACHOT 58A

PHRASE *Awaken to the good and give thanks.*

PRACTICE Find something that is good in every situation, and acknowledge it as good.

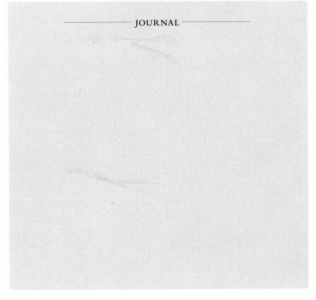

JOURNAL

ONE WHO RECOGNIZED the good that another did to him knows that his friend loves him. And "as in water, face reflects to face, so the heart of a person to a person," (Proverbs 27:19) gratitude awakens love. This is the great fundamental in the wisdom of character traits that gratitude brings one to love, which is why this quality is so central. Love without gratitude has no ability to endure.

—RABBI SHLOMO WOLBE (1914–2005)

PHRASE *Awaken to the good and give thanks.*

PRACTICE Find something that is good in every situation, and acknowledge it as good.

———————— JOURNAL ————————

GRATITUDE IS NOT JUST a nice gesture or a worthy personal quality. It is a real obligation like any other in the code of law. If you withhold it, you are a thief!

—RABBI YERUCHAM LEVOVITZ (1873–1936)

PHRASE *Awaken to the good and give thanks.*

PRACTICE Find something that is good in every situation, and acknowledge it as good.

JOURNAL

ENTHUSIASM

––––––

THE HEBREW TERM FOR "enthusiasm" (*zerizut*) translates as "alacrity," which suggests a liveliness or keen fervor. Acting with alacrity means springing forward without hesitation or obstacle. That does not mean that you are reckless or that your action is unpremeditated, but that no time is wasted, no rationalizations deflect you. Not only will alacrity lead to productivity, it unifies the action and the heart so that you and your doing become one.

> The fact that one is not lazy does not mean that he has acquired enthusiasm.
> —RABBI SHALOM NOACH BEREZOVSKY (1911–2000)

PHRASE *If not now, when?*

PRACTICE As soon as you are aware that you are awake, arise from the bed without a second's delay.

––––––– JOURNAL –––––––

THERE ARE PEOPLE WHO ARE intelligent and quick in a certain field of learning or in a certain craft but who lack ideas or experience in other fields. When faced with a situation with which they are unfamiliar, they think and reflect and ponder, and then they consult and think again interminably. In truth, this one's virtue is his problem. Because humans are intelligent, they can always find endless rationales that support different courses of action. Because of one's inability to reach a final decision, opportunity passes by, or one's hesitations delay an enterprise for days or years, thus sacrificing one's benefits for long periods of time.

—RABBI MENACHEM MENDEL LEFFIN (1749–1826)

PHRASE *If not now, when?*

PRACTICE As soon as you are aware that you are awake, arise from the bed without a second's delay.

JOURNAL

ENTHUSIASM

"THE DAY IS SHORT, the work formidable, the workers lazy, the wages high and the Boss impatient" (Pirkei Avot 2:15). Rabbi Tarfon is teaching that there is a fire deep within each of us that powers our desire to do. When that fire rages strong, we are productive, bold, even zealous in living. But there are times when the flames are dampened by confusion, exhaustion, or laziness. When our goals are clear and dedicated to good, it's up to us to stoke the fires of enthusiasm in our hearts.

—ALAN MORINIS (B. 1949)

PHRASE   *If not now, when?*

PRACTICE   As soon as you are aware that you are awake, arise from the bed without a second's delay.

JOURNAL

Week 28 Day 3

LIKE A BIRD, a person can reach undreamed-of heights as long as he works his wings. But if he relaxes them for but one minute, he plummets downward.

—RABBI YISRAEL SALANTER (1810–1883)

PHRASE *If not now, when?*

PRACTICE As soon as you are aware that you are awake, arise from the bed without a second's delay.

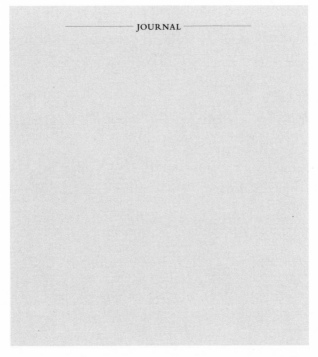

JOURNAL

SLOTH IS LIKE A SMALL tear in a garment that will destroy the whole thing if not attended to, or like a slight leak in a water pipe that might ultimately cause the whole house to flood.

—RABBI YECHIEL BEN YEKUTIEL (D. 1300)

PHRASE   *If not now, when?*

PRACTICE   As soon as you are aware that you are awake, arise from the bed without a second's delay.

JOURNAL

YOU MUST KNOW THAT the trait of enthusiasm is the foundation of all the traits. . . . The trait of enthusiasm is an ornament to all the other traits and it perfects all of them.

—*ORCHOT TZADDIKIM* (1540)

PHRASE   *If not now, when?*

PRACTICE   As soon as you are aware that you are awake, arise from the bed without a second's delay.

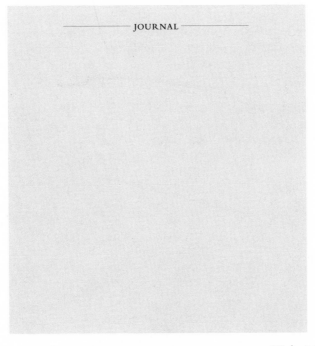

———— JOURNAL ————

THERE ARE MANY RATIONALES that a person uses to buttress and reinforce his laziness. The most common pretext to exempt oneself from fulfilling his obligations is the excuse that one lacks the requisite abilities to properly carry out one's tasks in life. . . . This holds true for every spiritual endeavor; supposed inability does not excuse anyone from any undertaking. If a person but gives his utmost, he will succeed.

—RABBI CHAIM SHMULEVITZ (1902–1979)

PHRASE *If not now, when?*

PRACTICE As soon as you are aware that you are awake, arise from the bed without a second's delay.

———————— JOURNAL ————————

JOY

———

EARTHLY PLEASURES and satisfactions bring many good feelings, but joy comes from a higher source. Because joy is a spiritual quality, it can arise independent of the worldly circumstances that happen to be present in someone's life at any given moment. And so the song-bird of joy is ready to sing within a person who is rich or poor, healthy or ailing, captive or free, as long as it is fed a diet of spiritual seeds.

A person who keeps to himself will find it difficult to be in a state of joy.
—RABBI ISRAEL MEIR KAGAN,
THE CHOFETZ CHAIM (1838–1933)

PHRASE *Mouth filled with laughter, lips with shouts of joy.*

PRACTICE Find the beauty in your day and allow it to open your heart to joy.

———— JOURNAL ————

JOY

THE DIVINE PRESENCE only dwells in a space where there is joy; the prophets did not experience prophecy whenever they desired. Instead, they would focus their consciousness, sit with joy and gladness in their hearts, and meditate, for prophecy does not come in the face of sadness or indolence, only where there is joy.

—RABBI ELIYAHU DE VIDAS (1518–1592)

PHRASE *Mouth filled with laughter, lips with shouts of joy.*

PRACTICE Find the beauty in your day and allow it to open your heart to joy.

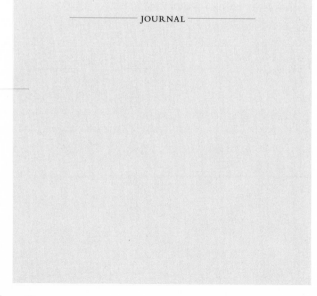

JOURNAL

PEOPLE SEARCH relentlessly for a "city of happiness"—
not realizing that it could only be found in a "state of
mind."

—RABBI AVRAHAM PAM (1913–2001)

PHRASE *Mouth filled with laughter, lips with shouts of joy.*

PRACTICE Find the beauty in your day and allow it
to open your heart to joy.

JOURNAL

JOY

ALL THE WORLD is a source of pleasure and beauty. Every detail of creation, every manifestation in matter, every movement in nature, can afford us immense pleasure. Man views the radiance of nature in a mass of colors. Should this not give him endless joy?

—RABBI NOSSON TZVI FINKEL, THE ALTER OF SLABODKA (1849–1927)

PHRASE *Mouth filled with laughter, lips with shouts of joy.*

PRACTICE Find the beauty in your day and allow it to open your heart to joy.

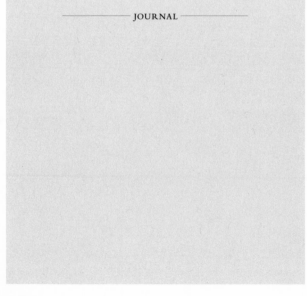

JOURNAL

OUR SAGES OF blessed memory have instructed us that man was created for the sole purpose of reveling in the Eternal and delighting in the splendor of the Divine Presence, this being the ultimate joy and the greatest of all pleasures in existence.

—RABBI MOSHE CHAIM LUZZATTO (1707–1746)

PHRASE   *Mouth filled with laughter, lips with shouts of joy.*

PRACTICE   Find the beauty in your day and allow it to open your heart to joy.

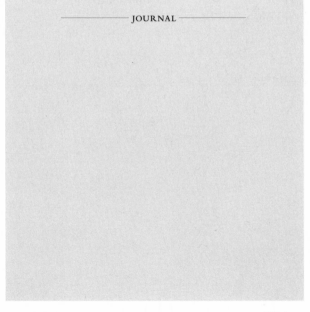

JOURNAL

JOY

A SENIOR STUDENT from a famous yeshiva in Poland visited the yeshiva of Rabbi Nosson Tzvi Finkel (1849–1927), the Alter of Slabodka. Several times, the Alter told the student to smile more. The student, who had been trained all his life to be serious and tense, could not change his habit and did not smile. Rabbi Nosson Tzvi regarded this as a serious character flaw, and he refused to allow his grandson to cross the border in the company of that student.

PHRASE   *Mouth filled with laughter, lips with shouts of joy.*

PRACTICE   Find the beauty in your day and allow it to open your heart to joy.

JOURNAL

DELIGHT AND JOY must accompany your every spiritual endeavor. Only when you delight and rejoice in each fine and positive deed will you have the enthusiasm to act in the most ideal manner and add to your deeds every day. Only when the delight and joy in your heart are bound to your fine and positive actions will they be anchored in you.

—RABBI ABRAHAM ISAAC KOOK (1865–1935)

PHRASE *Mouth filled with laughter, lips with shouts of joy.*

PRACTICE Find the beauty in your day and allow it to open your heart to joy.

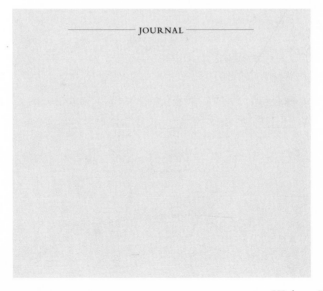

JOURNAL

STRENGTH

———

JEWISH TRADITION recognizes that human drives are natural to us, and are a source of our productive capacity. But our drives, like all sources of energy, are still potentially dangerous. A person of wisdom and strength is one who lives in mastery of his or her drives, rather than allowing those deep inner forces to rule as their master.

> It is taught: "A thirty-year-old achieves strength" (Pirkei Avot 5:21). We might think that this means physical strength, but it actually refers to strength of character, when the ability to fuse strength to purpose emerges.
> —RABBI CHAIM OF VOLOZHIN (1749–1821)

PHRASE *Strong as a lion, strong as the sun.*

PRACTICE Find your point of weakness and reinforce it.

———————— JOURNAL ————————

WHEN A PERSON FEELS that he is in great spiritual ruin, he should know that the opportunity has arrived to erect a new building, one that is more lofty and elevated, more stable and magnificent than what had been there previously. He must fortify himself and gather strength to improve his ways and deeds with proper order, a courageous heart, pure desire, and a heart filled with strength and inner joy.

—RABBI ABRAHAM ISAAC KOOK (1865–1935)

PHRASE   *Strong as a lion, strong as the sun.*

PRACTICE   Find your point of weakness and reinforce it.

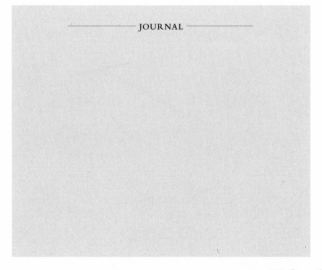

JOURNAL

STRENGTH

BEN ZOMA WOULD SAY: "Who is mighty? One who conquers his evil inclination" (Pirkei Avot 4:1). The strongest, most powerful force of the heart's might is the power to overcome the evil inclination. Courage in battle is not as great; there are many strong, brave warriors who have learned the arts of war and know how to fight. But the battle of the evil inclination demands much greater, more powerful, and more sophisticated force.

—RABBEINU YONAH OF GERONDI (D. 1263)

PHRASE *Strong as a lion, strong as the sun.*

PRACTICE Find your point of weakness and reinforce it.

JOURNAL

THE BASIS OF MUSSAR is to rethink and examine everything, even that which appears to be completely self-evident. We find in Pirkei Avot, "Who is strong?" (4:1). This inquiry itself teaches us—to ask. After we look deeper, we find that things are not as they originally appeared. The truth is, in fact, often the very opposite of the appearance. A strong person is one who conquers his inclination—not one who is a muscle-bound giant.

—RABBI AVRAHAM ZALMANES (D. 1944)

PHRASE   *Strong as a lion, strong as the sun.*

PRACTICE   Find your point of weakness and reinforce it.

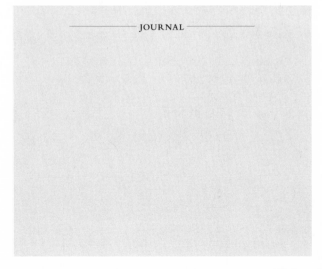

JOURNAL

YOU MUST KEEP IN MIND a fundamental principle of Torah and the service of the Almighty: without hard work, you will not accomplish anything. One must be a spiritual warrior to fend off every advancement of his evil inclination. A determined effort on one's part will earn the heavenly assistance needed to prevail. This is expressed homiletically in the Torah itself: "When you will go to war against your enemy, and the Lord your God will deliver him into your hand" (Deuteronomy 21:10). When one works actively at overcoming his negative desires and traits, then he is assured of the Heavenly assistance necessary to succeed. However, when one fails to do battle, then his *yetzer hara* (evil inclination) will get the better of him, even if he is as great a soul as Cain.

—RABBI ELIYAHU LOPIAN (1872–1970)

PHRASE *Strong as a lion, strong as the sun.*

PRACTICE Find your point of weakness and reinforce it.

JOURNAL

A KING HAD CUPS made of delicate glass. He said: "If I pour hot water into them, they will expand and burst; if cold water, they will contract and shatter." What did he do? He mixed hot and cold water, and poured it into them, and so they remained unbroken. Likewise, the Holy One said: "If I create the world with the attribute of mercy alone, its sins will be too many; if with strength alone, how could the world be expected to endure? So I will create it with both strength and mercy, and may it endure!"

—MIDRASH GENESIS RABBAH 12:15

PHRASE   *Strong as a lion, strong as the sun.*

PRACTICE   Find your point of weakness and reinforce it.

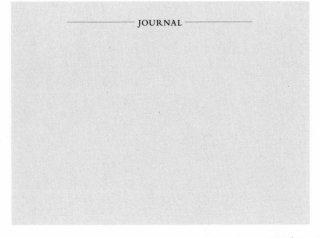

JOURNAL

STRENGTH

WHEN YOU LOVE GOD for His generous loving-kindness toward you and all the goodness He has bestowed upon you, you must not trust your righteousness, but rather fear a moment of weakness that might cause you to sin. This is total love, including both sides of the spectrum, for love can only be said to be perfect when combined with strength, and conversely, strength is only perfect when infused with love.

—RABBI ELIYAHU DE VIDAS (1518–1592)

PHRASE *Strong as a lion, strong as the sun.*

PRACTICE Find your point of weakness and reinforce it.

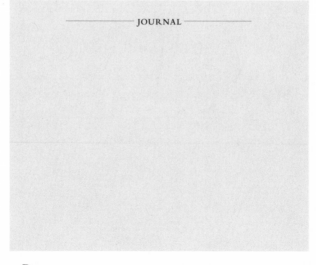

JOURNAL

LOVING-KINDNESS

—————

MANY PEOPLE DO ACTS of loving-kindness, yet more profound is the personality of loving-kindness. Each of us is capable of acts of benevolence, but someone who is a personality of loving-kindness makes care for others the axis around which his or her life revolves. This person is not content to wait for opportunities to do kindness for others, but seeks out ways to give and care and support, as if his or her life depended on it. For the personality of loving-kindness, it does.

A day should not pass without acts of loving-kindness, either with one's body, money, or soul.
—RABBI YESHAIAH HOROWITZ (1570–1626)

PHRASE *My world on selfless caring stands.*

PRACTICE Make a phone call, a visit, or send a card every day this week, as an act of loving-kindness.

————— JOURNAL —————

RABBI HAMA SON OF Rabbi Hanina said: "What does the text mean: 'Walk after the Eternal your God'? It means to walk after the attributes of the Holy One of Blessing. Just as God clothes the naked, so should you clothe the naked, as it is written: 'And the Eternal God made garments of skins for Adam and his wife and clothed them' (Genesis 3:21). Just as the Holy One of Blessing visited the sick, so should you also visit the sick, as it is written: 'And the Eternal appeared to him by the terebinths of Mamre [after Abraham's circumcision]' (Genesis 18:1). Just as the Holy One of Blessing comforted mourners, so should you also comfort mourners, as it is written: 'After the death of Abraham, God blessed his son Isaac' (Genesis 25:11). Just as the Holy One of Blessing buried the dead, so should you also bury the dead, as it is written: 'God buried him [Moses] in the valley' (Deuteronomy 34:6)."

—TALMUD, SOTAH 14A

PHRASE *My world on selfless caring stands.*

PRACTICE Make a phone call, a visit, or send a card every day this week, as an act of loving-kindness.

JOURNAL

THE CORNERSTONE SERVICE to God of Rabbi Nosson Tzvi Finkel [the Alter of Slabodka] was loving-kindness. To him, this meant being careful of another's honor and dignity, helping others, having one's heart overflow with kindness, and utilizing every opportunity to benefit others. It meant that older students should learn with younger ones. Above all, it meant that one should greet his fellow with a pleasant countenance, because it makes the other feel good and binds people together in friendship.

—RABBI CHAIM ZAITCHIK (1905–1989)

PHRASE *My world on selfless caring stands.*

PRACTICE Make a phone call, a visit, or send a card every day this week, as an act of loving-kindness.

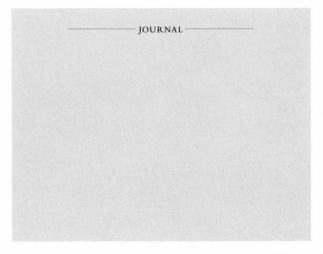

——————— JOURNAL ———————

IF YOU MAKE an effort to help everyone you meet, you will feel close to everyone. A stranger is someone you have not yet helped. Doing acts of kindness for everyone you can fill your world with friends and loved ones.

—RABBI ELIYAHU DESSLER (1892–1953)

PHRASE *My world on selfless caring stands.*

PRACTICE Make a phone call, a visit, or send a card every day this week, as an act of loving-kindness.

———————— JOURNAL ————————

ACTS OF LOVING-KINDNESS are greater than charity in three ways. Acts of loving-kindness can be done through personal action as well as with money, they can be given to rich and poor alike, they can be performed for both the living and the dead.

—TALMUD, SUKKAH 49B

PHRASE *My world on selfless caring stands.*

PRACTICE Make a phone call, a visit, or send a card every day this week, as an act of loving-kindness.

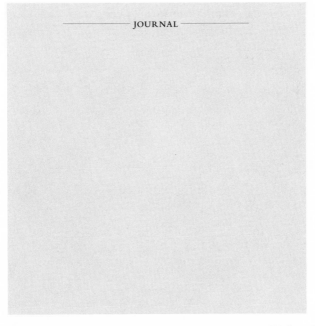

JOURNAL

LOVING-KINDNESS

A PERSON WHO WALKS the path of kindness will constantly be striving to give to others and express love. Even if he has achieved much in other areas he still chooses to make his world one of love and generosity. He makes every effort to love every person; he strives to help his fellow in every possible manner—in thought, speech, and deed. He constantly arouses the love that is in his heart.

—RABBI SHALOM NOACH BEREZOVSKY (1911–2000)

PHRASE *My world on selfless caring stands.*

PRACTICE Make a phone call, a visit, or send a card every day this week, as an act of loving-kindness.

JOURNAL

MOST PEOPLE ARE CONCERNED about their own material needs and another person's spirituality. It should be the other way around: a person is obligated to be concerned with his own spirituality and the material well-being of others. The material needs of my neighbor are my spiritual need.

—RABBI YISRAEL SALANTER (1810–1883)

PHRASE *My world on selfless caring stands.*

PRACTICE Make a phone call, a visit, or send a card every day this week, as an act of loving-kindness.

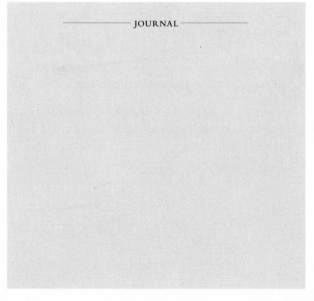

——————— JOURNAL ———————

ORDER

————

ORDER IS AN inner trait that rests on other traits. A person who is not punctual, for example, may be lacking in the trait of order; but in reality their problematic behavior has a deeper root, like perhaps laziness. On the other side of the spectrum, the deeper trait that causes a person to be overly strict in the rule of order might be a lack of trust in God. If order is an issue in a person's life, that person should peer deeply within to discover the root trait that is at the real heart of the matter.

> First a person should put his house together, then his town, then the world.
>
> —RABBI YISRAEL SALANTER (1810–1883)

PHRASE *First things first and last things later.*

PRACTICE In the places of disorder in your life, express your honor for whatever it is that could be kept in better order.

————— JOURNAL —————

THEY WERE VERY CAREFUL about being neat and orderly at the Mussar yeshiva in Kelm, Lithuania. Everything was clean and polished, with garbage pails in every
corner, so that the space would be clean. No one would
leave an object where it did not belong, nor move something from its proper place. It is said that someone once
left an umbrella in the yeshiva and many years later came
back and found it sitting in exactly the same place. The
Alter of Kelm, Rabbi Simcha Zissel Ziv (1824–1898),
once gave a Yom Kippur sermon about a pair of boots
that was not arranged properly in the entranceway.

PHRASE *First things first and last things later.*

PRACTICE In the places of disorder in your life, express your honor for whatever it is that could be
kept in better order.

JOURNAL

ORDER

KNOWING THAT THINGS are well arranged creates a feeling of inner satisfaction and confidence that everything is under control. Order helps you find things when you need them and saves you the time you would lose looking for them. Many things will only function if they are arranged correctly, like a machine that requires every one of its parts to be in good working order—and often in a specific sequence—to run properly.

—RABBI ELIYAHU DESSLER (1892–1953)

PHRASE *First things first and last things later.*

PRACTICE In the places of disorder in your life, express your honor for whatever it is that could be kept in better order.

——— JOURNAL ———

THE EVENING LITURGY contains the line, "Who orders the stars in their watches in the sky according to His Will." Specific order shows that the world has a Ruler, whether it is in His small building blocks, such as atoms and cells, or in the great celestial bodies, such as the sun and the moon. This order testifies to the Will that rules the world, the Will of the Creator. There is also a role for this connection between order and will in the small world, which is man, which he makes for himself in his life. If we see order in someone's work, we know that he is a person of strong will.

—RABBI SHLOMO WOLBE (1914–2005)

PHRASE *First things first and last things later.*

PRACTICE In the places of disorder in your life, express your honor for whatever it is that could be kept in better order.

——————— JOURNAL ———————

ORDER

WHEN THINGS ARE DONE in order, they will not be vulnerable to mistakes and confusion. And when they are not done in an orderly fashion, then there will constantly be mistakes.

—*SEFER HACHINUCH*, (13TH CENTURY)

PHRASE *First things first and last things later.*

PRACTICE In the places of disorder in your life, express your honor for whatever it is that could be kept in better order.

JOURNAL

Rabbi Simcha Zissel Ziv of Kelm (1824–1898) once went to visit his son at the yeshiva where he was studying. Before he sought out his son, he went to the boy's room, where he found all his possessions set out in good order. From this alone, he could tell that his son was doing well in yeshiva. Only then did he go to find his son.

PHRASE *First things first and last things later.*

PRACTICE In the places of disorder in your life, express your honor for whatever it is that could be kept in better order.

JOURNAL

ORDER

THE KNOT THAT TIES together a string of pearls is not the main part of the necklace, but should it come untied, the entire necklace falls apart. The knot guards the pearls from getting lost. So, too, with order. It is the knot that guards all of the good things in the world. If a person is organized, his study, prayer, and deeds are all safely guarded.

—RABBI YERUCHAM LEVOVITZ (1873–1936)

PHRASE *First things first and last things later.*

PRACTICE In the places of disorder in your life, express your honor for whatever it is that could be kept in better order.

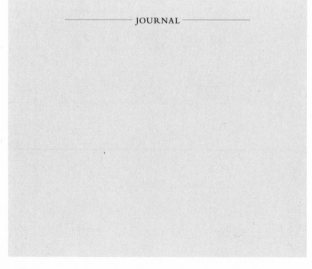

JOURNAL

EQUANIMITY

WHEN SOMEONE FALLS prey to the illusion that they are the sole master of their life, their inner experience will bounce up and down according to the degree to which reality happens to correspond to their wishes. In truth, there is no real basis for linking our happiness to the changing fortunes that feature in every life. The Mussar teachers counsel us to replace that win-lose mentality with an inner attitude of trust in the Creator.

> Despair is the worst of ailments. No worries are justified except: "Why am I so worried?"
> —RABBI YISRAEL SALANTER (1810–1883)

PHRASE *Rise above the good and the bad.*

PRACTICE When your mind is perturbed, look beyond the present moment, imagine the different feelings that lie ahead, and restore your balance.

JOURNAL

EQUANIMITY

A STUDENT ASKED a rabbi to take him as a disciple. The Master asked him, "My son, have you attained equanimity?" The student said, "Master, explain your words." The Master replied, "If one person honors you and the second insults you—are they equal in your eyes?" The student said, "No, my master. I feel pleasure from the person who honors me, and pain from the one who insults me." The Master said to the student, "Go in peace, my son. Until your soul does not feel honor when one honors you and embarrassment when one insults you, your consciousness is not ready to be attached to the supernal realm. So go and surrender your heart even more, a true surrendering, until you have attained equanimity."

—RABBI CHAIM VITAL (1543–1620)

PHRASE *Rise above the good and the bad.*

PRACTICE When your mind is perturbed, look beyond the present moment, imagine the different feelings that lie ahead, and restore your balance.

JOURNAL

THE HUMBLE PERSON finds serenity; one who seeks honor and recognition cultivates a life of inevitable frustration.

—RABBI CHAIM SHMULEVITZ (1902–1979)

PHRASE *Rise above the good and the bad.*

PRACTICE When your mind is perturbed, look beyond the present moment, imagine the different feelings that lie ahead, and restore your balance.

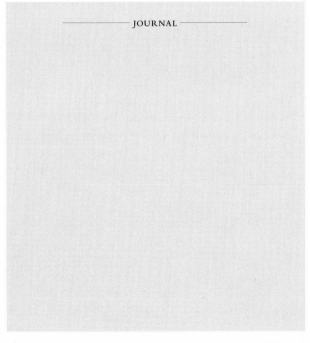

JOURNAL

GOD CREATED THE SOUL of man upright, happy in life, and enjoying tranquility in its feelings; any time that a person directs his life to the life of Nature in general, he will find happiness and gladness of heart: the sound of the song of the birds from among the branches that give forth song, the sight of the splendor of the Carmel and the Sharon with their beautiful flowers, the smell of the lilies and every delightful fruit that is in the Garden of HaShem, the Earth that He gave to man. These are the creations that restore a person to Nature, after he has become removed from it by the culture and society that distanced him.

—RABBI ABRAHAM ISAAC KOOK (1865–1935)

PHRASE *Rise above the good and the bad.*

PRACTICE When your mind is perturbed, look beyond the present moment, imagine the different feelings that lie ahead, and restore your balance.

JOURNAL

A PERSON WHO FEARS Heaven stands before the Creator of the universe, knowing that his task is to do His will. Nothing else is important, and therefore nothing else bothers him. In fear of Heaven there is perfect tranquility.

—RABBI HILLEL GOLDBERG (B. 1948)

PHRASE *Rise above the good and the bad.*

PRACTICE When your mind is perturbed, look beyond the present moment, imagine the different feelings that lie ahead, and restore your balance.

JOURNAL

EQUANIMITY

A PERSON WHO has gained peace of mind has gained everything. To obtain peace of mind, you need to be at peace with the people in your environment. You need to be at peace with yourself, with your emotions and desires. Furthermore, you need to be at peace with your Creator.

—RABBI SHLOMO WOLBE (1914–2005)

PHRASE *Rise above the good and the bad.*

PRACTICE When your mind is perturbed, look beyond the present moment, imagine the different feelings that lie ahead, and restore your balance.

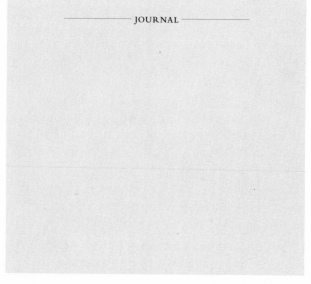

JOURNAL

AN UNCEASING INNER GAZE toward one's responsibility leads to remembrance, remembrance leads to concern, concern leads to confidence, confidence leads to strength, and strength leads to serenity and wholeness, internally and externally, in thought and in deed.

—RABBI AVRAHAM ELYA KAPLAN (1890–1924)

PHRASE *Rise above the good and the bad.*

PRACTICE When your mind is perturbed, look beyond the present moment, imagine the different feelings that lie ahead, and restore your balance.

JOURNAL

HONOR

———

THE ROOT OF THE Hebrew term for "honor" (*kavod*) means "heavy," which traches us two different lessons. On the one hand, the pursuit of prestige and recognition is a never-ending burden to the one who requires external validation of their own worth. On the other hand, the person who honors other people recognizes that another human being embodies a substantial spiritual reality. Every human being is a remarkable creation who merits honor on account of their "weight" in spiritual terms.

> Ben Zoma would say: "Who is honored? One who honors others."
>
> —PIRKEI AVOT 4:1

PHRASE *Every one, holy soul.*

PRACTICE Whether physically or just in your heart, bow to every human being you encounter.

———— JOURNAL ————

THE MORE LACKING ONE is in inner perfection, the more nature will seek to gain perfection on an outer level. It is only in a state of low-level spirituality that there will be aroused in a person a desire to glorify himself before others, both with the virtues he possesses and with others he does not possess.

—RABBI ABRAHAM ISAAC KOOK (1865–1935)

PHRASE *Every one, holy soul.*

PRACTICE Whether physically or just in your heart, bow to every human being you encounter.

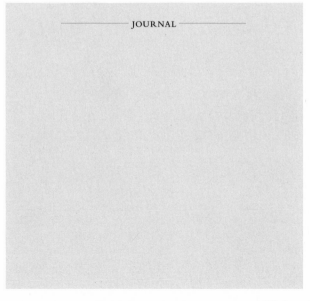

JOURNAL

HONOR

Joshua said: "Everyone should be under your suspicion as if he were a thief; but always show everyone respect as if he were like Rabban Gamaliel [head of the academy]."

—TALMUD, DERECH ERETZ RABBAH 25

PHRASE *Every one, holy soul.*

PRACTICE Whether physically or just in your heart, bow to every human being you encounter.

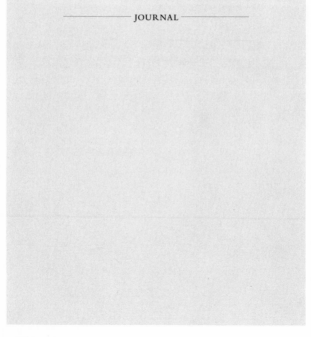

JOURNAL

"IF ONE PURSUES HONOR, it will elude him, but if one flees from honor, it will pursue him" (Talmud, Eruvin 13b). A man once approached his rabbi to ask how it was that he kept fleeing from honor and it somehow never caught up with him. "The trouble is," said his rabbi, "you keep looking back over your shoulder."

—IRVING BUNIM (1901–1980)

PHRASE *Every one, holy soul.*

PRACTICE Whether physically or just in your heart, bow to every human being you encounter.

JOURNAL

MOST POSITIVE TRAITS are only relevant to a person as regards himself. However, in his conduct with his fellow, he is obligated to employ the opposite virtue. For example, to flee from honor is a precious quality. However, the reverse is true concerning others, as the Sages said: "Who is honored? One who honors others" (Pirkei Avot 4:1).

—RABBI YISRAEL SALANTER (1810–1883)

PHRASE   *Every one, holy soul.*

PRACTICE   Whether physically or just in your heart, bow to every human being you encounter.

JOURNAL

OUR WORLD IS A WORLD of values. Everything has a value that can be seen in the price one is willing to pay for it. A person's labor, too, has value. And if a worker says, "I sell you my knowledge," he can demand a huge sum and there is no law of overcharging (Shulchan Arukh, Yoreh Dei'ah 336:3). Also, a person as a person has a value, but how can we estimate a person's value? It is impossible to measure out his value—so is there another way to estimate it? Yes: the honor others show them is a reliable measure of how they value them.

—RABBI SHLOMO WOLBE (1914–2005)

PHRASE *Every one, holy soul.*

PRACTICE Whether physically or just in your heart, bow to every human being you encounter.

JOURNAL

HONOR

RABBI ELIEZER the son of Shamua would say: "The honor of your student should be as precious to you as your own; the honor of your colleague, as the honor of your master; and the honor of your master as your awe of Heaven."

—PIRKEI AVOT 4:12

PHRASE *Every one, holy soul.*

PRACTICE Whether physically or just in your heart, bow to every human being you encounter.

———— JOURNAL ————

HUMILITY

THE CAUSE OF much suffering can be traced back to issues of ego. The Mussar teachers find ego lurking behind anger, as the source of impatience, and so on. The Talmud goes so far as to equate egotism with idolatry. This is not just a convenient metaphor; there is room for only one deity on the altar of our lives, and if we elevate ego to that rank, then we provide no place for God at the center. Being egotistical is not *like* idolatry; it *is* idolatry. And humility is the antidote.

> The essence of humility is in a person's not attaching importance to himself for any reason whatsoever.
> —RABBI MOSHE CHAIM LUZZATTO (1707–1746)

PHRASE *No more than my space, no less than my place.*

PRACTICE To practice humility, never be the first to speak. Alternatively, to stretch into your space, speak up more readily.

——— JOURNAL ———

HUMILITY IS A NOBLE TRAIT and a good quality, the opposite of pride. One who possesses this trait has already spared his soul many kinds of evils, and one who has attained this honored state is performing a divine commandment and receives reward to the extent of his humility.

—*ORCHOT TZADDIKIM* (1540)

PHRASE *No more than my space, no less than my place.*

PRACTICE To practice humility, never be the first to speak. Alternatively, to stretch into your space, speak up more readily.

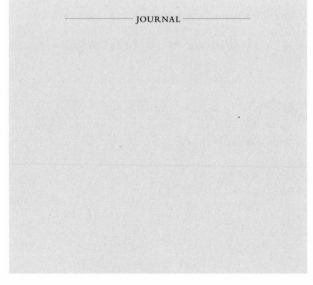

JOURNAL

WITH THE ABILITY to take lessons from the world around us, there is no room for the concept of pride! If I do something good, I can fall prey to taking pride in it. But if I take it as a lesson about how to do something positive—I didn't do anything that warrants pride, for I am only taking a lesson! And when I am operating from a position of taking lessons, I am always inclined to see how the action could have been improved.

—RABBI SHLOMO WOLBE (1914–2005)

PHRASE *No more than my space, no less than my place.*

PRACTICE To practice humility, never be the first to speak. Alternatively, to stretch into your space, speak up more readily.

———— JOURNAL ————

WHEN WE'RE CONVERSING with someone, do we spend the whole time searching for launching points for what we want to say? Or, do we actually listen to appreciate what they are trying to relate? The first stance is the hubris of believing that what we have to say and contribute is primary; certainly my insight is brighter, my interpretation more inspiring, and my perspective more valuable. The root of the Hebrew word for humility (*anava*) is *la'anot,* which means "to answer." When the humble person speaks, he participates as one component of the whole. He truly responds.

—RABBI MICHA BERGER (B. 1965)

PHRASE *No more than my space, no less than my place.*

PRACTICE To practice humility, never be the first to speak. Alternatively, to stretch into your space, speak up more readily.

———————— JOURNAL ————————

TRUE WISDOM CANNOT DWELL in the proud-hearted, nor will they ever achieve the ultimate, which is pure understanding, because they are too proud to go to sages and learned ones.

—RABBI BAHYA IBN PAQUDA (11TH CENTURY)

PHRASE *No more than my space, no less than my place.*

PRACTICE To practice humility, never be the first to speak. Alternatively, to stretch into your space, speak up more readily.

———— JOURNAL ————

AND GOD SAID, "Let us make man in our image, after our likeness." Who is the "us" in this verse? The angels. Even though the angels did not assist God in His creation, Scripture did not hesitate to teach proper conduct and the trait of humility, that a great person should consult with and receive permission from a lesser one.

—RASHI TO GENESIS 1:26

PHRASE *No more than my space, no less than my place.*

PRACTICE To practice humility, never be the first to speak. Alternatively, to stretch into your space, speak up more readily.

JOURNAL

ONE WHO DENIES one's strengths is not humble, but rather a fool. Rather, a humble person is one who understands that all his strengths and accomplishments are a gift from heaven. The more a person recognizes this, the more humble he is.

—RABBI LEIB CHASMAN (1867–1931)

PHRASE *No more than my space, no less than my place.*

PRACTICE To practice humility, never be the first to speak. Alternatively, to stretch into your space, speak up more readily.

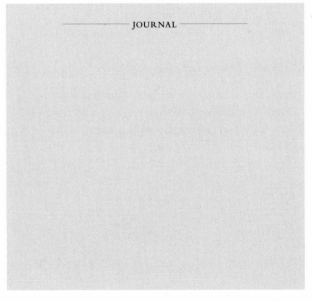

JOURNAL

GENEROSITY

WHEN YOU ENCOURAGE your hand to open, you strengthen the quality of generosity in your heart. Jewish thought tells us that our spiritual lives center on relationships—between a person and his or her own soul, with other people, and with God. Being generous enhances the key relationships in your life, even with yourself; it is actually a key process in creating those relationships. Give to whom you would love.

> If you want to bond yourself to loving your friend, give to him for his benefit.
>
> —TALMUD, DERECH ERETZ ZUTA 2

PHRASE *The generous heart gives freely.*

PRACTICE Do a different kind of generous act every day—one day with money, one day with time, one day with caring, one day with possessions, and the like.

JOURNAL

WHEN GOD CREATED MAN, He made him a giver and a taker. The power of giving is a higher power of the traits of the Creator of all, blessed be He, who has mercy, does good, and gives without receiving anything in exchange. Thus He made man, as it is written, "In the image of God He made man," for man is able to have mercy, do good, and give.

—RABBI ELIYAHU DESSLER (1892–1953)

PHRASE   *The generous heart gives freely.*

PRACTICE   Do a different kind of generous act every day—one day with money, one day with time, one day with caring, one day with possessions, and the like.

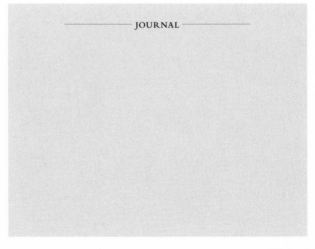

JOURNAL

GENEROSITY

A PERSON CANNOT be considered generous unless he is willing to give, regardless of the season of the year or the time of day.

—*ORCHOT TZADDIKIM* (1540)

PHRASE   *The generous heart gives freely.*

PRACTICE   Do a different kind of generous act every day—one day with money, one day with time, one day with caring, one day with possessions, and the like.

———— JOURNAL ————

MANY TIMES I HAVE seen a person pass a synagogue, and the people inside call out to him, "Holy! Holy! Please come in and join us!" But I have yet to see a person pass by a house where a meal is being served, and the people eating at the table call out to the passerby, "Feast! Feast! Please come inside and join us!"

—RABBI YISRAEL SALANTER (1810–1883)

PHRASE   *The generous heart gives freely.*

PRACTICE   Do a different kind of generous act every day—one day with money, one day with time, one day with caring, one day with possessions, and the like.

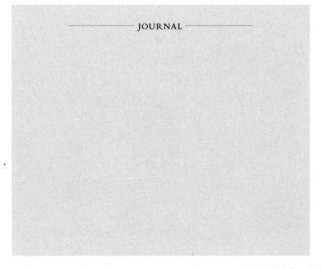

JOURNAL

RABBI NECHUNYA ben Hakanah was asked by his disciples how he had merited such a long life. He answered them: "I never sought honor at the expense of my fellow, I never went to sleep without forgiving anyone who might have offended or injured me that day, and I was always generous with my money."

—TALMUD, MEGILLAH 28A

PHRASE   *The generous heart gives freely.*

PRACTICE   Do a different kind of generous act every day—one day with money, one day with time, one day with caring, one day with possessions, and the like.

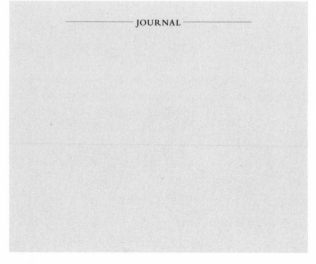

JOURNAL

IF A PERSON GIVES to another all the good gifts of the world but does so with a grumpy demeanor, the Torah regards it as if he had given nothing. But if he receives his neighbor cheerfully and kindly, the Torah regards it as if he had given him all the good gifts of the world.

—AVOT DE RABBI NATHAN 23B

PHRASE *The generous heart gives freely.*

PRACTICE Do a different kind of generous act every day—one day with money, one day with time, one day with caring, one day with possessions, and the like.

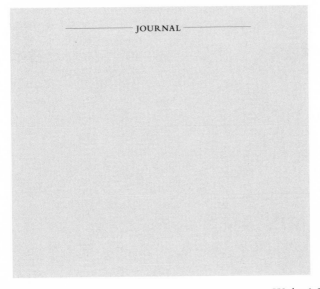

JOURNAL

GENEROSITY

RABBI YITZHAK TEACHES: "Whoever gives even a small coin to a poor person receives six blessings, but whoever accompanies his coins with kind words of reassurance receives eleven blessings."

—TALMUD, BAVA BATRA 9B

PHRASE *The generous heart gives freely.*

PRACTICE Do a different kind of generous act every day—one day with money, one day with time, one day with caring, one day with possessions, and the like.

———— JOURNAL ————

WATCHFULNESS

————

THIS WORLD is as real as can be, and the actions we take here have real significance. The path we are walking is wide enough to run and dance, but the precipices and drops are real as well. And in life, if you don't pay careful attention to where you put your feet, you are likely to fall. Should we hunker down in fear? Not at all. We ought to go through life as energetically and gracefully as a dancer or skater in full flight, while being just as watchful as they would be of every step we take.

> The caution one exerts is proportional to one's spiritual level.
>
> —RABBI MORDECHAI MILLER (1921–2001)

PHRASE *Bright light of mind on the steps ahead.*

PRACTICE With every step, be careful where you put your feet (physically and metaphorically).

———— JOURNAL ————

WATCHFULNESS

IF A PERSON UNBLINDS himself, the Holy One helps him, and he is saved from the evil inclination. But if he does not do so, the Holy One will certainly not superintend him.

—RABBI MOSHE CHAIM LUZZATTO (1707–1746)

PHRASE *Bright light of mind on the steps ahead.*

PRACTICE With every step, be careful where you put your feet (physically and metaphorically).

JOURNAL

THE SEISMOGRAPH HAS TAUGHT us that a tremor in any part of the world can be felt by a sufficiently sensitive instrument everywhere in the world. The same is true of a person's deeds. One should not think that his actions do not affect others. Everything one does in some way affects everyone else in the world.

—RABBI YERUCHAM LEVOVITZ (1873–1936)

PHRASE   *Bright light of mind on the steps ahead.*

PRACTICE   With every step, be careful where you put your feet (physically and metaphorically).

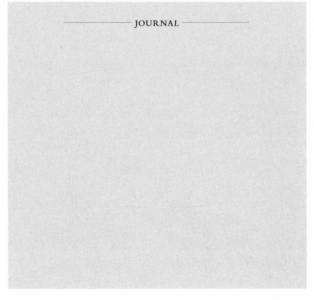

JOURNAL

WATCHFULNESS

WHY IS IT THAT when there is ice on the streets, everyone walks slowly and carefully out of fear of slipping physically, while in their daily lives, people are not afraid of slipping spiritually?

—RABBI ISSER ZALMAN MELTZER (1870–1953)

PHRASE *Bright light of mind on the steps ahead.*

PRACTICE With every step, be careful where you put your feet (physically and metaphorically).

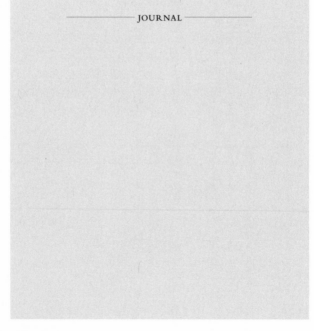

JOURNAL

SATAN'S POWER RESIDES in rushing man to carry out an action right away, before he stops to consider and wonder about what he is doing. The deed is done and there he stands, deliberating after the fact.

—RABBI YOSEF YOZEL HURWITZ,
THE ALTER OF NOVARDOK (1849–1919)

PHRASE *Bright light of mind on the steps ahead.*

PRACTICE With every step, be careful where you put your feet (physically and metaphorically).

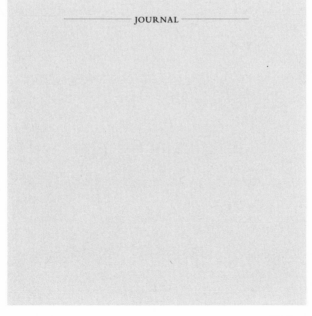

JOURNAL

WATCHFULNESS

IN THE HEBREW, "caution" connotes watching and overseeing, and hints at a separate presence above things observing, which is symbolic of the self watching itself and taking note.

—RABBI YAAKOV FELDMAN (B. 1950)

PHRASE *Bright light of mind on the steps ahead.*

PRACTICE With every step, be careful where you put your feet (physically and metaphorically).

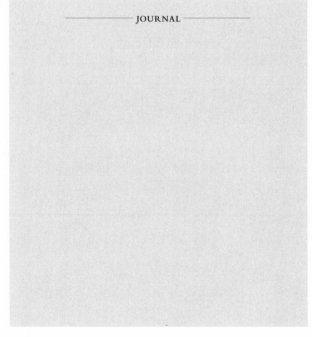

——————— JOURNAL ———————

A PERSON'S NATURAL STATE is one of complete awareness and concern for the ramifications of each of his
actions. Only one who possesses a certain degree of cru-
elty to himself can stifle this instinctive drive to be concerned about his actions.

—RABBI A. HENACH LEIBOWITZ (1918–2008)

PHRASE *Bright light of mind on the steps ahead.*

PRACTICE With every step, be careful where you put
your feet (physically and metaphorically).

——————— JOURNAL ———————

JUDGING OTHERS FAVORABLY

———

JUDGE OTHERS AS YOU would have them judge you. The least you would want is to be treated with honesty and objectivity. Beyond that, you surely would want to see compassion in the eyes of another person looking your way, because you know that your heart means well even if your hands and tongue stumble. The core practice in learning to judge others as you would be judged is to seek out a positive reason that explains why someone is doing something that seems so patently wrong.

> Our Sages taught: anyone who judges his peer on the merit-side of the scales of justice, they judge him to be meritorious.
> —TALMUD, SHABBAT 127B

PHRASE *There's another side to the story.*

PRACTICE Take every opportunity to give people the benefit of the doubt.

———— JOURNAL ————

EVERY INNER TRAIT has its role. Warped logic, for example, is useful because no matter how clear-cut another's wrongdoing might appear, a person can draw on this ability to find justification for their actions rather than leap to negative conclusions.

—RABBI NOSSON TZVI FINKEL,
THE ALTER OF SLABODKA (1849–1927)

PHRASE *There's another side to the story.*

PRACTICE Take every opportunity to give people the benefit of the doubt.

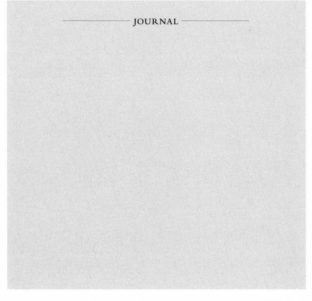

JOURNAL

"LOVE YOUR NEIGHBOR as yourself" (Leviticus 19:18). This shows us that it is inappropriate for there to be any separation between a person and his friend. One must judge his friend on the side of merit, just the same way we judges ourselves.

—RABBI AVRAHAM SABBA (1440–1508)

PHRASE *There's another side to the story.*

PRACTICE Take every opportunity to give people the benefit of the doubt.

JOURNAL

A MAN CAME BEFORE the king and said to him, "I am going to ask of you something I first asked of the Creator. If you do it, I will praise God and thank you. If you do not do it, I will praise God and thank Him, and judge you favorably, that you were not the one He chose to be His messenger."

—RABBI SHLOMO BEN YEHUDAH
(10TH–11TH CENTURIES)

PHRASE *There's another side to the story.*

PRACTICE Take every opportunity to give people the benefit of the doubt.

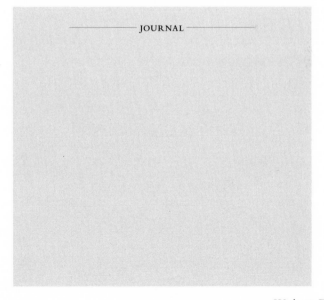

JOURNAL

JUDGING OTHERS FAVORABLY

IF A MAN HAS BOILS, the fly will ignore the rest of the body and sit on the boil. Thus it is with someone who gossips. He overlooks all the good in a person and speaks only of the evil.

—*ORCHOT TZADDIKIM* (1540)

PHRASE *There's another side to the story.*

PRACTICE Take every opportunity to give people the benefit of the doubt.

——————— JOURNAL ———————

AFTER THE RABBIS TESTED Abba the surgeon by stealing his rugs and then trying to sell them back to him, they admitted, "They are yours. We removed them from your house. Please tell us what you suspected of us in this?" He replied: "I said to myself: 'Perhaps the rabbis needed money to redeem captives, and that you were ashamed to ask me for them outright.'"

—TALMUD, TA'ANIT 21B

PHRASE *There's another side to the story.*

PRACTICE Take every opportunity to give people the benefit of the doubt.

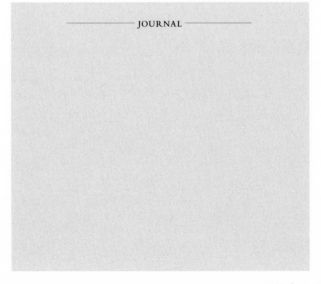

JOURNAL

JUDGING OTHERS FAVORABLY

SOMEONE WHO WANTS to be greater than others should not dig a pit for his friend; rather he should build a hill for himself.

—RABBI YISRAEL SALANTER (1810–1883)

PHRASE   *There's another side to the story.*

PRACTICE   Take every opportunity to give people the benefit of the doubt.

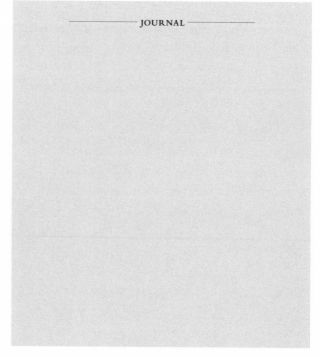

——————— JOURNAL ———————

CALMNESS

JEWISH TRADITION identifies being slow to anger as a quality of God. In the Mussar teachings, anger is not considered an inherently negative characteristic but it is surely counter to holy aspirations to lash out in anger without some measure of reflection. Being *slow* to anger gives a person the time and space needed to consider how to respond, and so spares him or her all the unfortunate outcomes that acting rashly tends to bring.

> The words of the wise are stated gently. In being good, do not be called evil.
> —RABBI MENACHEM MENDEL LEFFIN (1749–1826)

PHRASE *Still waters of the heart.*

PRACTICE Any time you become angry, ask yourself: "What is it that is making me sad?"

JOURNAL

CALMNESS

H<small>E WHO TEARS</small> his clothes, breaks his utensils, or scatters his money in anger should be, in your eyes, as one who serves idols. For such are the workings of the evil inclination. Today he says to you, "Do this," and tomorrow, "Do the other," until the point is reached when he says to you, "Serve idols," and you will go and do it.

—TALMUD, SHABBAT 105B

PHRASE *Still waters of the heart.*

PRACTICE Any time you become angry, ask yourself: "What is it that is making me sad?"

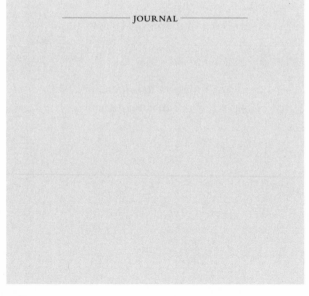

JOURNAL

ANGER IS A DESTRUCTIVE soul-trait. Just as scurvy is a disease of the body, so is anger a disease of the soul.

—*ORCHOT TZADDIKIM* (1540)

PHRASE *Still waters of the heart.*

PRACTICE Any time you become angry, ask yourself: "What is it that is making me sad?"

JOURNAL

CALMNESS

THE TORAH IDEAL is to speak to others in a manner that makes it a pleasurable experience. Your tone of voice should be calm and pleasant when you speak to anyone. Do not speak in anger or raise your voice.

—RABBI ELIYAHU LOPIAN (1872–1970)

PHRASE   *Still waters of the heart.*

PRACTICE   Any time you become angry, ask yourself: "What is it that is making me sad?"

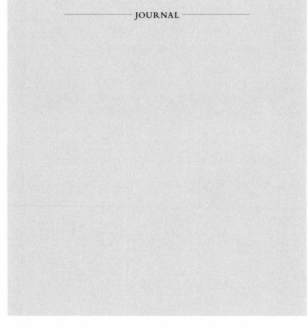

JOURNAL

RABBI CHANINA BEN DOSA would say: "Anyone who calms his fellow's soul also calms God's spirit. But someone who does not calm his fellow's soul, neither is God's spirit calmed by him."

—PIRKEI AVOT 3:13

PHRASE   *Still waters of the heart.*

PRACTICE   Any time you become angry, ask yourself: "What is it that is making me sad?"

JOURNAL

CALMNESS

"You shall surely rebuke your neighbor" (Leviticus 19:17) is a commandment, but someone who cannot rebuke gently, without hurting the other's feelings, is free from the obligation to rebuke.

—RABBI CHAIM OF VOLOZHIN (1749–1821)

PHRASE *Still waters of the heart.*

PRACTICE Any time you become angry, ask yourself: "What is it that is making me sad?"

JOURNAL

ONE WHO DOES NOT lose control of his temper is a beloved of God.

—TALMUD, PESACHIM 113A

PHRASE *Still waters of the heart.*

PRACTICE Any time you become angry, ask yourself: "What is it that is making me sad?"

JOURNAL

PATIENCE

————

Is PATIENCE A VIRTUE? We are all familiar with the negative effects of impatience, but failure to take action can be just as big a spiritual obstacle. In both cases, it is likely that the person fails to see their own responsibility. Impatient people are certain that their fuming reactivity has nothing to do with them, while others rationalize their inactivity by calling it patience. Patience is about responsibility—for your emotional response to situations, and for the situations themselves.

> Wait—and be saved like a bird from a snare;
> Hurry, and usher your soul to despair.
> —YOSEF QIMHI (C. 1160–1235)

PHRASE *Every person has their hour, everything its place.*

PRACTICE Whenever you are forced to wait, fill the space with a positive activity, such as resting or singing or reviewing something you learned.

———— JOURNAL ————

EVEN THOUGH ENTHUSIASM is extremely praiseworthy, one must be careful not to be overly hasty in his service, for one who rides too quickly is very apt to stumble, and one who runs too quickly falls. And things cannot be done correctly in haste, but only with patience.

—*ORCHOT TZADDIKIM* (1540)

PHRASE *Every person has their hour, everything its place.*

PRACTICE Whenever you are forced to wait, fill the space with a positive activity, such as resting or singing or reviewing something you learned.

JOURNAL

THERE WERE TEN GENERATIONS from Adam to Noah. This teaches us the extent of God's tolerance; for all these generations angered Him, until He brought upon them the waters of the Flood. There were ten generations from Noah to Abraham. This teaches us the extent of God's tolerance; for all these generations angered Him, until Abraham came and reaped the reward for them all.

—PIRKEI AVOT 5:2

PHRASE *Every person has their hour, everything its place.*

PRACTICE Whenever you are forced to wait, fill the space with a positive activity, such as resting or singing or reviewing something you learned.

———— JOURNAL ————

PATIENCE IS A WONDERFUL VIRTUE. Make an effort to be gentle and forbearing with insulting and aggravating people and with your family. Be as strong as a lion to control your tongue even if you are burning with the desire to speak your mind. "A word is worth one gold piece; silence is worth two" (Talmud, Megillah 18a).

—RABBI ELIEZER PAPO (1785–1826)

PHRASE *Every person has their hour, everything its place.*

PRACTICE Whenever you are forced to wait, fill the space with a positive activity, such as resting or singing or reviewing something you learned.

—— JOURNAL ——

PATIENCE

Woe to the pampered one who has never been trained to be patient. Either today or in the future he is destined to sip from the cup of affliction.

—RABBI MENACHEM MENDEL LEFFIN (1749–1826)

PHRASE   *Every person has their hour, everything its place.*

PRACTICE   Whenever you are forced to wait, fill the space with a positive activity, such as resting or singing or reviewing something you learned.

JOURNAL

A RABBI ONCE VISITED Rabbi Yisrael Salanter and found him depressed because he had just gotten angry at someone. "Did you give vent to your anger?" "God forbid," Rabbi Yisrael replied, "only I was aware of it." "Then why so upset?" Rabbi Yisrael was surprised, "Don't you know that giving vent to anger is tantamount to idolatry, and that puts one in the grip of all forms of Hell?"

—RABBI DOV KATZ (1900–1979)

PHRASE *Every person has their hour, everything its place.*

PRACTICE Whenever you are forced to wait, fill the space with a positive activity, such as resting or singing or reviewing something you learned.

———— JOURNAL ————

PATIENCE

ACCORDING TO HIS ABILITY—this is a great principle in serving God. Yes, a person must have a lot of patience with himself.

—RABBI SHLOMO WOLBE (1914–2005)

PHRASE   *Every person has their hour, everything its place.*

PRACTICE   Whenever you are forced to wait, fill the space with a positive activity, such as resting or singing or reviewing something you learned.

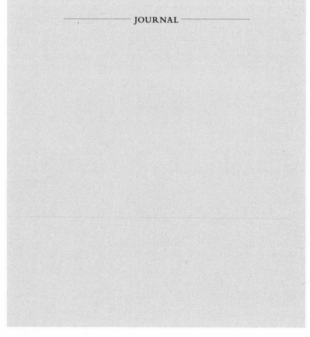

JOURNAL

LOVE

WHAT WE CALL LOVE is actually a deep interweaving of beings. The emotion we feel is actually a marker that the other person or thing has become part of ourselves; we are no longer separate from the other. This explains why losing someone or something we love hurts so much. It is not just "as if" something has been torn from us. When we enter love, a part of ourselves merges with the other and when we lose love, a part of ourselves is torn away.

> Love in the soul of the righteous embraces all creatures, it excludes nothing, and no people or tongue.
> —RABBI ABRAHAM ISAAC KOOK (1865–1935)

PHRASE *Love the One and love His works.*

PRACTICE Express your love to those who are closest to you.

———— JOURNAL ————

LOVE

THE TORAH DEMANDS love for man because man is God's creature, made in His image, because man's origin is God. This being so, you must love not only the unfortunate and tormented, but even the well fed and the haughty.

—RABBI NOSSON TZVI FINKEL,
THE ALTER OF SLABODKA (1849–1927)

PHRASE *Love the One and love His works.*

PRACTICE Express your love to those who are closest to you.

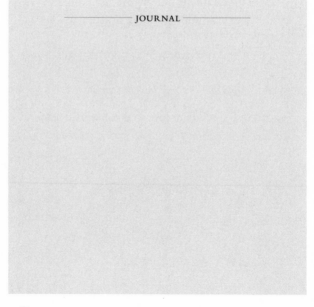

JOURNAL

FEAR WITHOUT LOVE—surely there is here a deficiency of love; love without fear—there is nothing here at all.

—RABBI YITZCHAK HUTNER (1906–1980)

PHRASE *Love the One and love His works.*

PRACTICE Express your love to those who are closest to you.

———— JOURNAL ————

TODAY ALL EDUCATION of children has to be done with love. Wherever children are educated, in the home, in every primary school, in every yeshiva—everywhere there is education—know this, that today education is only with love. Students and children have to feel the love of their parents and their teacher.

—RABBI SHLOMO WOLBE (1914–2005)

PHRASE   *Love the One and love His works.*

PRACTICE   Express your love to those who are closest to you.

JOURNAL

AND WHAT IS LOVE? It is the completion of the soul, and it pulling itself toward the Creator so that one can cleave to the Supernal Light. Such a soul is the source of knowledge, and it is pure and refined.

—*ORCHOT TZADDIKIM* (1540)

PHRASE *Love the One and love His works.*

PRACTICE Express your love to those who are closest to you.

JOURNAL

LOVE AND AWE dwell in the heart and the soul: they are within you, and you do not need to ask them from another, but from yourself.

—RABBI ELIYAHU DE VIDAS (1518–1592)

PHRASE *Love the One and love His works.*

PRACTICE Express your love to those who are closest to you.

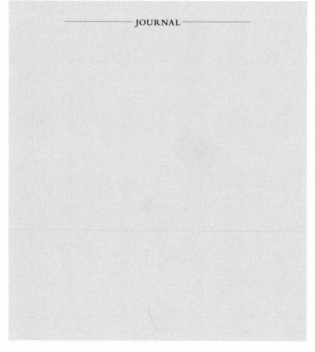

JOURNAL

THE DISCIPLES OF Rabbi Chaim Friedlander (1923–1986) noticed that he had a warm smile on his face even when he spoke to someone on the phone. Someone asked him, "The other person can't see your smile, so why bother?" Rabbi Friedlander responded: "Although the listener may not be able to see my smile, he can hear my smile."

PHRASE   *Love the One and love His works.*

PRACTICE   Express your love to those who are closest to you.

JOURNAL

ABSTINENCE

ABSTAINING FROM something can feel to us like incurring a loss, because we are denying ourselves something that is available to us. This sense of loss in the present needs to be weighed against the gain that will come in the future. The one who practices right abstention becomes master of his or her own desires. That mastery gives rise to a tremendous feeling of liberation because there is joy in being freed from enslavement to our never-ending desires.

> If you abuse wine [*tirosh*] you will become *rash*—poor. If you use it rightly, you will become *rosh*—a leader.
>
> —TALMUD, YOMA 76B

PHRASE *Learn to say no and be holy.*

PRACTICE Choose one drive or urge and decline to indulge it.

JOURNAL

WHY DO HUMAN BEINGS have cravings over and above their physical needs? It must be that God implanted these unnecessary cravings in us as a challenge. They give us an opportunity to exercise self-control, which is what enables us to rise to the highest spiritual levels.

—RABBI ELIYAHU DESSLER (1892–1953)

ABSTINENCE

PHRASE *Learn to say no and be holy.*

PRACTICE Choose one drive or urge and decline to indulge it.

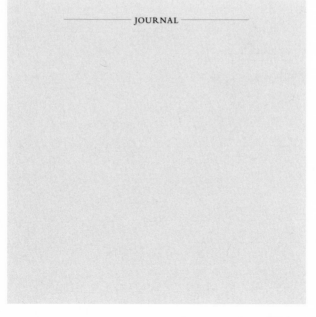

JOURNAL

ABSTINENCE

EVALUATE THE DEGREE to which your heart clings to the love of this world and examine the prior habits that allowed the trappings of this world to taint you. Then, if your ambition inspires you toward this great matter and lofty trait, you should gradually change those habits and loosen your bonds with this world little by little.

—RABBI AVRAHAM BEN HARAMBAM (1186–1237)

PHRASE *Learn to say no and be holy.*

PRACTICE Choose one drive or urge and decline to indulge it.

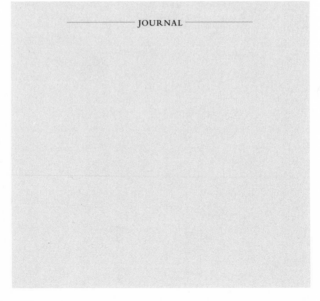

——— JOURNAL ———

MORE DESIRABLE THAN anything else in respect to the attainment of abstinence is solitude. For when one removes worldly goods from before his eyes, he removes desire for them from his heart.

—RABBI MOSHE CHAIM LUZZATTO (1707–1746)

PHRASE *Learn to say no and be holy.*

PRACTICE Choose one drive or urge and decline to indulge it.

———————— JOURNAL ————————

ABSTINENCE

THE TRAIT OF ABSTINENCE on the part of man in regard to this world is commendable only if employed in its place. That is to say, if forbidden food or sexual intercourse or wealth present themselves to him, he should make full use of this trait so that it will restrain him from these things.

—SA'ADIA GAON (892–942)

PHRASE *Learn to say no and be holy.*

PRACTICE Choose one drive or urge and decline to indulge it.

JOURNAL

BEFORE A PERSON gives up his portion in the next world for others, let's see if he is willing to forgo some of his share in this world for others.

—RABBI YOSEF YOZEL HURWITZ,
THE ALTER OF NOVARDOK (1849–1919)

PHRASE *Learn to say no and be holy.*

PRACTICE Choose one drive or urge and decline to indulge it.

JOURNAL

WHAT INCLINES ONE'S nature to pleasures to the extent that he requires so much strength and scheming to separate himself from them is the gullibility of the eyes, their tendency to be deceived by good and pleasing superficial appearances.

—RABBI MOSHE CHAIM LUZZATTO (1707–1746)

PHRASE *Learn to say no and be holy.*

PRACTICE Choose one drive or urge and decline to indulge it.

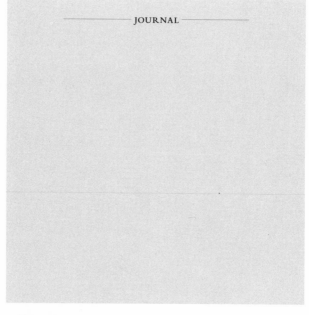

JOURNAL

COMPASSION

———

COMPASSION IS A reaching out to give to the other, based on the divine essence in you recognizing the divine soul in the other. Whether that person has earned your care, or is even worthy of it, is not relevant to acts of compassion. An open heart peers beyond superficial realities to perceive the very essence of another person. That deep dimension of the other to which the heart responds compassionately is the soul (*neshama*), which is made in the image and likeness of God.

> Compassion is the foundation of belief. For a person who isn't compassionate, even the belief in God is a kind of idolatry.
>
> —RABBI YISRAEL SALANTER (1810–1883)

PHRASE *Care for the other—we are one.*

PRACTICE See the part of you that lives within the other, and take care.

——— JOURNAL ———

ONE WINTER, Rabbi Yisrael Salanter (1810–1883) donned a fur coat and went to the home of miserly rich man. The man invited the rabbi in, but the rabbi remained in the doorway and launched into a lengthy Talmudic discourse. The host began to shiver and his teeth to chatter. As his lips turned blue and he was about to faint, he persuaded the rabbi to enter the warm house. Rabbi Yisrael continued: "The students in the yeshiva are freezing. We need money for fuel. Now that you feel what they feel, I am sure you will help me." As long as he lived, the wealthy man provided fuel for the study hall.

PHRASE *Care for the other—we are one.*

PRACTICE See the part of you that lives within the other, and take care.

JOURNAL

ONE'S COMPASSION SHOULD extend to all creatures, and one should neither despise nor destroy them, for the wisdom above extends to all of creation—inanimate objects, plants, animals, and humans.

—RABBI MOSHE CORDOVERO (1522–1570)

PHRASE   *Care for the other—we are one.*

PRACTICE   See the part of you that lives within the other, and take care.

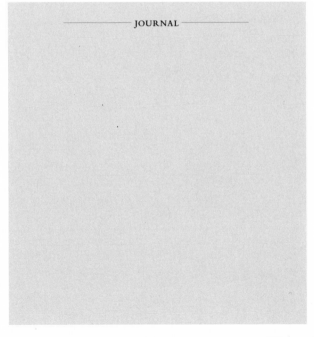

JOURNAL

COMPASSION IS AN EXTREMELY noble soul-trait. Anything that one can do to cultivate this soul-trait, one should exert oneself to do. Just as one wishes to receive compassion in one's own time of need, so too, one should pity others when they are in need. As it is written: "And you should love your neighbor as yourself" (Leviticus 19:18).

—*ORCHOT TZADDIKIM* (1540)

PHRASE   *Care for the other—we are one.*

PRACTICE   See the part of you that lives within the other, and take care.

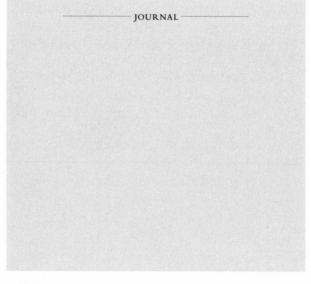

JOURNAL

Samuel the Small taught: "When your enemy falls, do not rejoice; when he stumbles, let your heart not be gladdened (Proverbs 24:17–18). Lest God see, and it will be displeasing in His eyes, and He will turn His wrath from him to you."

—PIRKEI AVOT 4:19

PHRASE *Care for the other—we are one.*

PRACTICE See the part of you that lives within the other, and take care.

——— JOURNAL ———

COMPASSION

RABBI LEIB CHASMAN (1867–1931) once saw a boy in the dining room eating fish with gusto, saying, "I love fish!" "If you really love fish," the Mussar teacher asked him, "why are you eating it? Shouldn't you be feeding it and ensuring that it's comfortable?"

PHRASE *Care for the other—we are one.*

PRACTICE See the part of you that lives within the other, and take care.

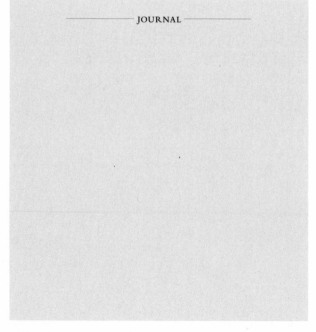

JOURNAL

WHOEVER IS COMPASSIONATE to his fellow is certainly of the children of our father Abraham, and whoever is not compassionate to his fellow is certainly not of the children of our father Abraham.

—TALMUD, BEITZAH 32B

PHRASE *Care for the other—we are one.*

PRACTICE See the part of you that lives within the other, and take care.

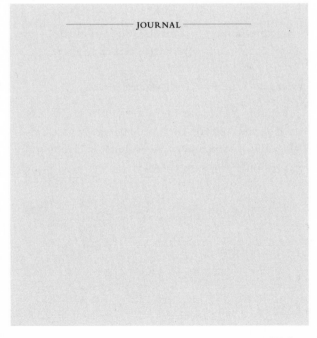

———— JOURNAL ————

MODESTY

IT HAS BEEN CENTURIES since someone came up with
a new way to make a mess of a human life. Innovation
isn't needed, since qualities like lust, dishonesty, anger,
and envy do the job so well. Ranking high among these
tried-and-true life disrupters is the power of lust. The
practice of modesty recognizes the true power of sexual
desire, and seeks to curb its expression, so that our personal and professional lives can be productive and happy.

There is nothing so dear to God as modesty.
—MIDRASH PESIKTA RABBATI 185B

PHRASE *Wise privacy bestows dignity.*

PRACTICE When you find yourself in a situation in
which you could reveal something—body, idea, feeling, information, and so on—commit to dignity and
reveal only what is necessary.

JOURNAL

RABBI ELAZAR SAID: Walking modestly with your God refers to attending to funerals and bringing a bride to a joyous wedding. Understand! If we are told to perform these commandments, which are normally done in public, with a modest walk, how much more so those generally performed in private!

—TALMUD, SUKKAH 49B

PHRASE *Wise privacy bestows dignity.*

PRACTICE When you find yourself in a situation in which you could reveal something—body, idea, feeling, information, and so on—commit to dignity and reveal only what is necessary.

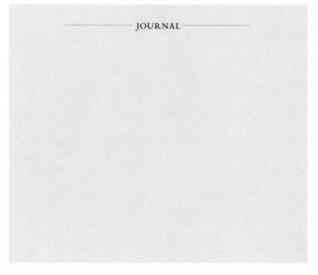

JOURNAL

EVEN WHEN YOU ARE in the most private room and no one can see you, still "walk modestly with your God" since His glory fills the entire world.

—RABBI SHABTAI SHEFTEL HOROWITZ (1590–1660)

PHRASE   *Wise privacy bestows dignity.*

PRACTICE   When you find yourself in a situation in which you could reveal something—body, idea, feeling, information, and so on—commit to dignity and reveal only what is necessary.

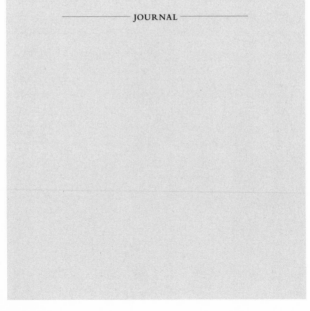

JOURNAL

DRESSING IN MODEST CLOTHING (respectable, but not outstanding), you will find that humility will slowly enter and penetrate your heart.

—RABBI MOSHE CHAIM LUZZATTO (1707–1746)

PHRASE *Wise privacy bestows dignity.*

PRACTICE When you find yourself in a situation in which you could reveal something—body, idea, feeling, information, and so on—commit to dignity and reveal only what is necessary.

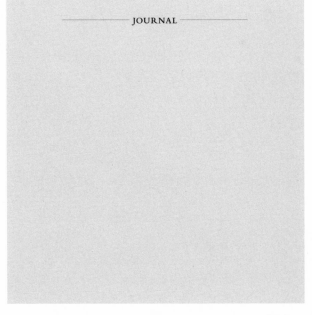

JOURNAL

MODESTY

GOD HAS TOLD YOU, person, what is good and what the Lord expects from you. But to perform justice, to love kindness, and walk modestly with your God.

—MICAH 6:8

PHRASE *Wise privacy bestows dignity.*

PRACTICE When you find yourself in a situation in which you could reveal something—body, idea, feeling, information, and so on—commit to dignity and reveal only what is necessary.

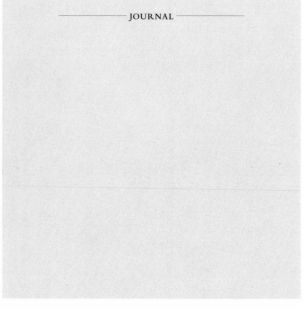

JOURNAL

MODESTY AT A WEDDING means rejoicing fully in the singing, dancing, and feasting while inwardly striving to direct all of those activities for the happiness of the wedding couple, not for oneself.

—RABBI NOSSON TZVI FINKEL,
THE ALTER OF SLABODKA (1849–1927)

PHRASE *Wise privacy bestows dignity.*

PRACTICE When you find yourself in a situation in which you could reveal something—body, idea, feeling, information, and so on—commit to dignity and reveal only what is necessary.

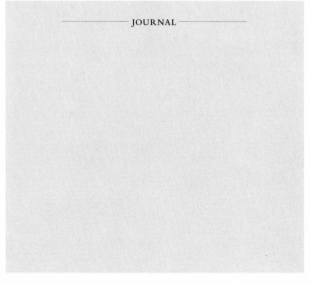

JOURNAL

MODESTY

A PERSON'S BEHAVIOR should be decent in private as well as in public.

—RABBI ABRAHAM TWERSKI (B. 1930)

PHRASE *Wise privacy bestows dignity.*

PRACTICE When you find yourself in a situation in which you could reveal something—body, idea, feeling, information, and so on—commit to dignity and reveal only what is necessary.

JOURNAL

WILLINGNESS

THE WILL YOU EXPRESS in life should not be your own. Attune to the divine will, and then make that higher purpose your own. The presence of the divine will is not hard to detect: be willing, but only to do things that represent truth (because tradition calls truth the "seal" of the Divine) and that foster goodness and kindness (because tradition tells us that God is good and does good, and that God's kindness endures forever).

> Rabban Gamliel would say: "Do His will like your will, in order that He will do your will like His will."
>
> —PIRKEI AVOT 2:4

PHRASE *The whole heart steps forward.*

PRACTICE When a difficulty arises, willingly lean into it rather than resisting or avoiding.

— JOURNAL —

WILLINGNESS

WHEN YOU DO what you want—your will—you do it willingly and eagerly. This is how you should do God's will as well. Do not differentiate between God's will and your own; make them one and the same. In other words, whatever you do, do in a manner that will be pleasing before God.

—RABBEINU YONAH OF GERONDI
TO PIRKEI AVOT 2:4(D. 1263)

PHRASE   *The whole heart steps forward.*

PRACTICE   When a difficulty arises, willingly lean into it rather than resisting or avoiding.

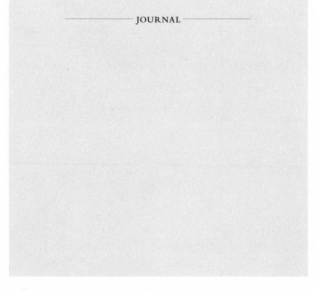

———— JOURNAL ————

RABBI AKIVA SAID: "All my life I wondered when I could love God 'with all your soul,' (Deuteronomy 6:5) even if He takes my life. Now the opportunity has come, I will fulfill it with joy."

—TALMUD, BERACHOT 61B

PHRASE *The whole heart steps forward.*

PRACTICE When a difficulty arises, willingly lean into it rather than resisting or avoiding.

——— JOURNAL ———

WILLINGNESS

THE ONLY WAY TO PREPARE ourselves for the coming of the Messiah is to reduce selfishness to a minimum, and so make ourselves willing receptacles for the Divine Light.

—RABBI ELIYAHU DESSLER (1892–1953)

PHRASE *The whole heart steps forward.*

PRACTICE When a difficulty arises, willingly lean into it rather than resisting or avoiding.

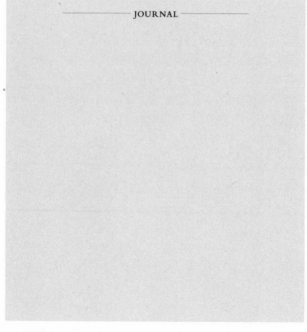

JOURNAL

EACH CREATURE WAS CREATED "willingly." Rashi explains: "They were asked if they wished to be created and they said, yes."

—TALMUD, ROSH HASHANAH 11A

PHRASE *The whole heart steps forward.*

PRACTICE When a difficulty arises, willingly lean into it rather than resisting or avoiding.

JOURNAL

314

THE ASCENSION OF the mountain of God must take place step by step. It is impossible to leap from the bottom to the top in one bound, nor is there any sense or profit in standing stationary on one spot in the valley, merely gazing at the mountain. One must walk, ascend, and continue to ascend without stopping.

—RABBI ELIYAHU LOPIAN (1872–1970)

PHRASE *The whole heart steps forward.*

PRACTICE When a difficulty arises, willingly lean into it rather than resisting or avoiding.

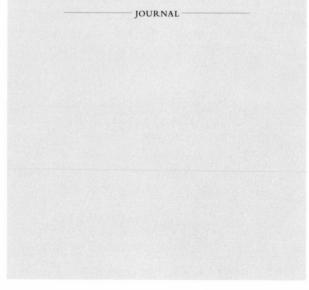

——— JOURNAL ———

HILLEL THE ELDER SAYS: "The place that my heart holds dear, that's the place where my feet will lead me."

—TALMUD, MOED KATAN 4:2

PHRASE *The whole heart steps forward.*

PRACTICE When a difficulty arises, willingly lean into it rather than resisting or avoiding.

———— JOURNAL ————

SIMPLICITY

CONSUMPTION HAS BEEN turned from a necessity into the very purpose for which life exists. Since no gratification endures for more than a brief time, the pursuit of inner well-being via consumption is a project doomed to failure. The Mussar teachings in this area encourage us to limit our devotion to accumulation and gratification to life's necessities. This approach may be countercultural, but it is much more likely to help us find the fulfillment we seek.

A poor person with his stale bread can be as much of a hedonist as a wealthy person with his feast.
—RABBI YISRAEL SALANTER (1810–1883)

PHRASE   *Rejoice in my portion.*

PRACTICE   Reduce spending to only what is necessary.

———— JOURNAL ————

IF PEOPLE WOULD only be satisfied with the essentials and if they'd only try to improve everyone else's well-being and share in their common concerns, they'd conquer the world and have more than they ever wanted from it.

—RABBI BAHYA IBN PAQUDA (11TH CENTURY)

PHRASE *Rejoice in my portion.*

PRACTICE Reduce spending to only what is necessary.

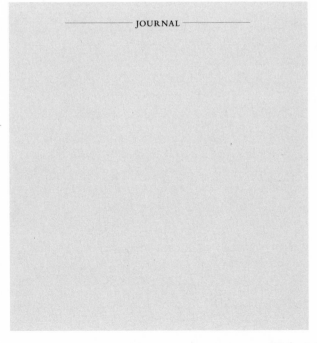

JOURNAL

318

SIMPLICITY

"THE MORE POSSESSIONS, the more worries" (Pirkei Avot 2:7). Do not think that your wealth and property will allow you to live happily and well. On the contrary—you will be caught up in taking care of them all year round. Any intelligent person can tell you that this is so, and any wealthy person can confirm it.

—RABBEINU YONAH OF GERONDI (D. 1263)

PHRASE *Rejoice in my portion.*

PRACTICE Reduce spending to only what is necessary.

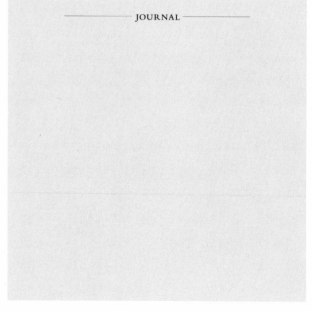

JOURNAL

EVERY DAY A HEAVENLY voice declares, "The whole world is provided with food because of the merit of Chanina, my son, who is satisfied with a measure of carobs from one Shabbat to another" (Talmud, Berachot 17B). The text does not say, "and Chanina has a measure of carobs," rather, it says, "and Chanina is satisfied with a measure of carobs." The crucial element is that he is satisfied with what he has.

—RABBI YIZCHAK BLAZER (1840–1907)

PHRASE *Rejoice in my portion.*

PRACTICE Reduce spending to only what is necessary.

JOURNAL

A VISITOR TO THE APARTMENT of the Chofetz Chaim, Rabbi Israel Meir Kagan (1838-1933), was struck by its sparseness. "Where is your furniture?" the man asked. "Where is yours?" replied the Chofetz Chaim. "Oh, I am only passing through," said the man. To which the Chofetz Chaim replied, "I also am just passing through."

PHRASE *Rejoice in my portion.*

PRACTICE Reduce spending to only what is necessary.

JOURNAL

WHEN SOMEONE SEES his neighbor acquiring some worldly property, whether some kind of food or clothing, or a house, or accumulating money, he works hard to get the same, because he thinks, "If my friend has this, I should also have it!"

—*ORCHOT TZADDIKIM* (1540)

PHRASE   *Rejoice in my portion.*

PRACTICE   Reduce spending to only what is necessary.

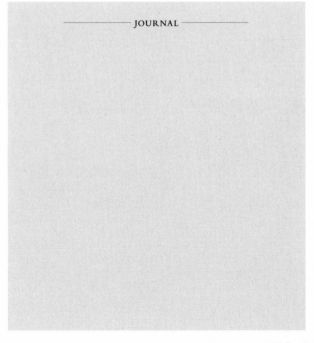

———— JOURNAL ————

SIMPLICITY

"WHEN YOU EAT of the labor of your hands, you are praiseworthy and all is well with you" (Psalms 128:2). "You are praiseworthy"—in this world; "and all is well with you"—in the world to come.

—PIRKEI AVOT 4:1

PHRASE *Rejoice in my portion.*

PRACTICE Reduce spending to only what is necessary.

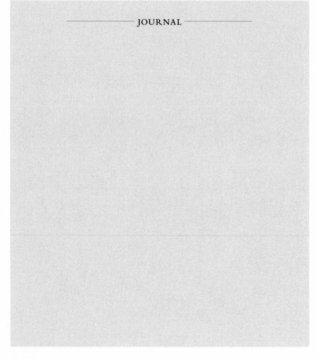

JOURNAL

COURAGE

BEING OF STRONG HEART should not be confused with being reckless. The courageous person may take a risk, but it will be calculated. The measure that is applied is not whether the action has a high likelihood of success. Indeed, it may not. Rather the deciding criterion is whether something absolutely needs to be done. If the step is that necessary, then bravery consists in not being deflected from doing that thing, whatever the outcome.

> Cowardice and egotism simply love company.
> —RABBI ELYAKIM KRUMBEIN (B. 1951)

PHRASE *Forward and upward, strong heart.*

PRACTICE Do the right thing without fear of the consequences.

JOURNAL

COURAGE

KNOW THAT TRUTH and righteousness are the ornaments of the soul, and they provide the individual with everlasting courage and confidence.

—RABBI MOSHE BEN MAIMON, THE RAMBAM (1135–1204)

PHRASE   *Forward and upward, strong heart.*

PRACTICE   Do the right thing without fear of the consequences.

JOURNAL

WHEN YOU GO OUT to battle against your enemies, and see horses, and chariots, and a people more numerous than you, be not afraid of them; for the Lord your God is with you, who brought you out of the land of Egypt.

—DEUTERONOMY 20:1

PHRASE *Forward and upward, strong heart.*

PRACTICE Do the right thing without fear of the consequences.

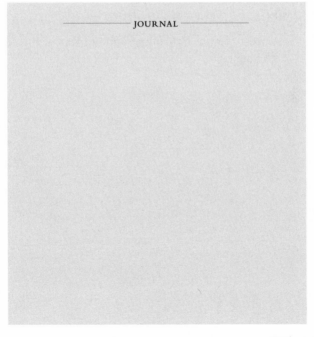

———— JOURNAL ————

Week 47, Day 3

IN THE CHAOS OF 1914, a group of rioters in Minsk grabbed a student from the Novardok yeshiva, stripped him almost naked and brought him to the house of Rabbi Moshe Mordechai Epstein, demanding a huge ransom. When the rabbi told them that he had no money, they took the student into the street to be shot. Rabbi Moshe Mordechai held his head, gathered his courage, walked into the street and began to shout and scream. A crowd gathered. Guns were pointed this way and that, but as the crowd grew, the gangsters melted away.

PHRASE *Forward and upward, strong heart.*

PRACTICE Do the right thing without fear of the consequences.

———————— JOURNAL ————————

WHEN THE SPIRIT IS EXHAUSTED—when memory revives the shadows of the past and their chill penetrates the heart—during such depressing moments of spiritual exhaustion, I am wont to picture before me, in my imagination, the exalted image of man: Wandering in the desert waste, alone on a globe that hurtles through infinite expanses, alone—alone he strives with courage—forward! And upward! In the path of victory over the secrets of Heaven and Earth—forward and upward!

—RABBI AVRAHAM ELYA KAPLAN (1890–1924)

PHRASE   *Forward and upward, strong heart.*

PRACTICE   Do the right thing without fear of the consequences.

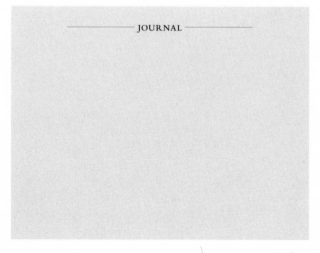

JOURNAL

COURAGE

Look to the Lord, be strong and of good, heartfelt courage! Look to the Lord.

—PSALMS 27:14

PHRASE *Forward and upward, strong heart.*

PRACTICE Do the right thing without fear of the consequences.

———— JOURNAL ————

WHEN I ASKED for Your help, You answered my prayer and gave me courage.

—PSALMS 138:3

PHRASE *Forward and upward, strong heart.*

PRACTICE Do the right thing without fear of the consequences.

————————— JOURNAL —————————

TRUST

It's NATURAL TO WORRY about oneself and one's future because we are motivated by our survival instinct. Yet our Mussar teachers call on us to live by higher principles than mere survival. The antidote they prescribe to loosen the clutches of self-interest is to practice trust. Trust is the quality that breaks down the barriers that keep us from connecting and giving to others. In the end, we create more resources for ourselves through generosity, and so our kind acts serve ourselves as well as others.

> When I am afraid, I will put my trust in You.
>
> —PSALMS 56:3

PHRASE *I rest in the hands of my Maker.*

PRACTICE Stretch into the territory of risk, not recklessly, but with trust.

JOURNAL

IF YOU DO NOT TRUST GOD, you will inevitably trust someone or something else. God will then put you under the care of the one you trust, rather than His own.

—RABBI BAHYA IBN PAQUDA (11TH CENTURY)

PHRASE *I rest in the hands of my Maker.*

PRACTICE Stretch into the territory of risk, not recklessly, but with trust.

JOURNAL

THE TRUSTING PERSON can turn away from all of life's problems, for he knows that he will not want. What he must provide for the needs of the body, he does in peace and contentment, for he knows that no one can take away what the Creator allotted to him. In times of danger, he does not tremble. He walks securely and does not fear for tomorrow, for as long as he relies on the Almighty, he has everything.

—RABBI YOSEF YOZEL HURWITZ,
THE ALTER OF NOVARDOK (1849–1919)

PHRASE *I rest in the hands of my Maker.*

PRACTICE Stretch into the territory of risk, not recklessly, but with trust.

JOURNAL

AT TIMES, A PERSON must tell himself or herself not to lose heart but rather maintain trust that HaShem will provide. However, we should be quicker to employ this concept regarding our own problems than when approaching the trials confronted by others. If we see a person in distress, we should make great efforts to help him without preaching to him about the virtues of trust.

—RABBI YECHEZKEL LEVENSTEIN (1895–1974).

PHRASE *I rest in the hands of my Maker.*

PRACTICE Stretch into the territory of risk, not recklessly, but with trust.

JOURNAL

TRUST

THE WAY WE SEE THINGS makes all the difference. See your happiness and success as coming from the heavens, and it will come from the heavens. See your happiness and success coming from the earth, and you will search for it here on earth. The Jews in the desert lived on bread that fell from heaven. But surely bread that comes from the earth is as much of a miracle. The answer is the above idea. Since they turned their eyes to the heavens, they received their nourishment from the heavens.

—RABBI ELIYAHU LOPIAN (1872–1970)

PHRASE *I rest in the hands of my Maker.*

PRACTICE Stretch into the territory of risk, not recklessly, but with trust.

JOURNAL

ONE WHO CHOOSES to ignore wisdom and is willing to place himself in danger is not displaying trust but rather recklessness.

—RABBI MOSHE CHAIM LUZZATTO (1707–1746)

PHRASE *I rest in the hands of my Maker.*

PRACTICE Stretch into the territory of risk, not recklessly, but with trust.

JOURNAL

A PERSON WHO truly trusts in God is truly rich. But a person who is only reputed to trust in God is like a person who is only reputed to be rich.

—RABBI YISRAEL SALANTER (1810–1883)

PHRASE *I rest in the hands of my Maker.*

PRACTICE Stretch into the territory of risk, not recklessly, but with trust.

JOURNAL

FAITH

The Hebrew noun *emuna* is translated as "faith" but really means "trust, confidence, reliability, faithfulness." The Torah does not command belief in God, but rather describes faith in HaShem, which is a striving to know and understand God's ways, of obeying His laws. We are given a sense, then, that faith is not believing, in the sense of deciding whether God exists or not, but rather a matter of expressing conviction. The act of faith is not proving but being faithful. As Psalms 18:25 says, "To the faithful you show yourself faithful."

I place God before me always.

—PSALMS 16:8

PHRASE   *Cleave to the One and be whole.*

PRACTICE   Say prayers daily.

JOURNAL

FAITH

ONE CAN TRAIN ONESELF to be occupied with faith. One can get used to saying at every opportunity, "Thank God," "If God wills," and so on.

—RABBI ELIYAHU DESSLER (1892–1953)

PHRASE *Cleave to the One and be whole.*

PRACTICE Say prayers daily.

——— JOURNAL ———

YOUR MOST POWERFUL SOURCE of help in acquiring faith is not to fear any evil, but instead, to accept all that happens to you with joy, much like a servant who knows that his master is open-hearted and has a generous eye.

—RABBI ELIYAHU DE VIDAS (1518–1592)

FAITH

PHRASE *Cleave to the One and be whole.*

PRACTICE Say prayers daily.

JOURNAL

FAITH

IT IS TRUE THAT FAITH rests on reason and there is solid evidence present to support faith. But such faith can be shaken. It is but a stage on the way to firm faith— the faith that is a firm bar of steel that cannot be eroded.

—RABBI YERUCHAM LEVOVITZ (1873–1936)

PHRASE *Cleave to the One and be whole.*

PRACTICE Say prayers daily.

JOURNAL

FAITH HAS MANY LEVELS. The level you are on depends on how intensely you live and feel your faith—how real and alive it is to you. Concomitantly, your level of faith dictates the demands the Almighty will place on you and what expectations He has of you.

—RABBI ZEIDEL EPSTEIN (1908–2007)

PHRASE *Cleave to the One and be whole.*

PRACTICE Say prayers daily.

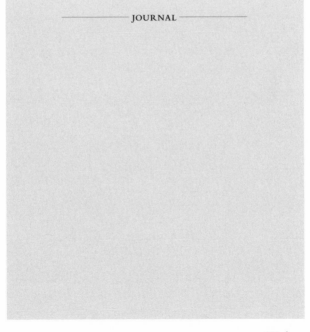

—————— JOURNAL ——————

FAITH

ONE WHOSE FAITH in God is firm and perfect, so that he trusts in God, automatically possesses ease of mind, and a happy life both here and in the hereafter.

—RABBI ELIYAHU LOPIAN (1872–1970)

PHRASE *Cleave to the One and be whole.*

PRACTICE Say prayers daily.

JOURNAL

TRUE BELIEF MEANS giving oneself over to God, trusting in Him totally and never doubting Him, no matter what the circumstances. This is the concept of faith—to cling to Him completely and unequivocally. Such attachment brings a person to complete wholeness.

—RABBI YEHUDAH LOEW,
MAHARAL OF PRAGUE (1525–1609)

PHRASE *Cleave to the One and be whole.*

PRACTICE Say prayers daily.

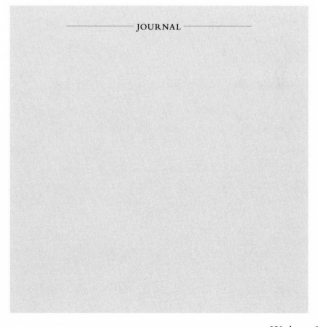

JOURNAL

TRUTH

———

WHAT COULD POSSIBLY cause you to vary from the truth? Survival would be one reason, but in ordinary life, the impulse to swerve from the truth is not easily justified. Nor is it innocent. Probe your motivations and you will encounter some other trait—like envy or laziness—seeking its own satisfaction. You deviate from truth when some inner trait wants to bend reality to its own purpose, but you will pay the ultimate price. The traits in question are your spiritual curriculum.

Keep distant from falsehood.

—EXODUS 23:7

PHRASE *Truth stands forever; falsehood has no legs.*

PRACTICE Check in with yourself before you speak any words, asking yourself: "Is this the truth?"

——— JOURNAL ———

Truth is one of the very foundations upon which the world stands. As this is so, when you speak falsely it is as if you are nudging at the world's foundation.

—RABBI MOSHE CHAIM LUZZATTO (1707–1746)

PHRASE *Truth stands forever; falsehood has no legs.*

PRACTICE Check in with yourself before you speak any words, asking yourself: "Is this the truth?"

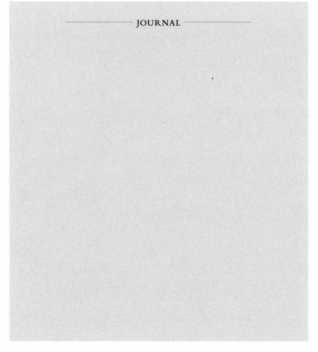

JOURNAL

TRUTH

PREFER DEATH TO a lying word,
for the ripple-effect of its plunder is worse.
When a man dies, he dies alone—
but many are slain with the lie and its curse.

—AVRAHAM IBN HASDAI (C. 915–990)

PHRASE   *Truth stands forever; falsehood has no legs.*

PRACTICE   Check in with yourself before you speak
any words, asking yourself: "Is this the truth?"

JOURNAL

Rabbi Elya Meir Bloch (dean of Telshe Yeshiva) had the urge to immerse himself in the Sea of Galilee. He removed his clothing and began to walk toward the water. His startled companion asked: "Why go to all the trouble? Who's to stop you from saying you swam in this sea?" Reb Elya Meir was astonished by the question. "It used to be said, If you can tell the truth why tell a lie? Now people say, If you can tell a lie, why bother with the truth?"

—RABBI CHAIM DOV KELLER (B. 1930)

PHRASE   *Truth stands forever; falsehood has no legs.*

PRACTICE   Check in with yourself before you speak any words, asking yourself: "Is this the truth?"

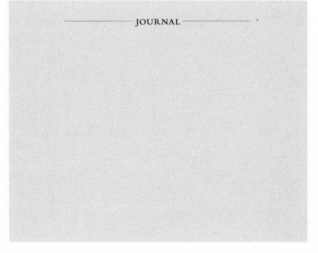

JOURNAL

TRUTH

THE LESS WE EXPAND ourselves—in money, power, time, and ego—the more space can be permeated with truth.

—RABBI MORDECHAI MILLER (1921–2001)

PHRASE *Truth stands forever; falsehood has no legs.*

PRACTICE Check in with yourself before you speak any words, asking yourself: "Is this the truth?"

——————— JOURNAL ———————

ANYONE WHO HAS PREJUDICES and whose perceptions are colored by self-interest will never see the truth in any area in which his bias operates. Only when his bias is removed will he be able to understand the truth.

—RABBI ELIYAHU DESSLER (1892–1953)

PHRASE *Truth stands forever; falsehood has no legs.*

PRACTICE Check in with yourself before you speak any words, asking yourself: "Is this the truth?"

JOURNAL

TRUTH

THE LIP OF TRUTH shall be established forever; but a lying tongue is but for a moment.

—PROVERBS 12:19

PHRASE *Truth stands forever; falsehood has no legs.*

PRACTICE Check in with yourself before you speak any words, asking yourself: "Is this the truth?"

JOURNAL

SILENCE

SILENCE IS A VIRTUE, but not always, just as speech is a strength, but not always. The wisdom of Mussar comes in identifying that the trait itself has no positive or negative valence—it gets its charge from the "measure" of the trait as it lives within us. We move ourselves in the direction of wholeness by becoming masters of both ends of the spectrum, so that we are just as capable of remaining silent when silence is what is called for as we are able to speak up when speaking is the right thing to do.

> A word is worth one gold piece; silence is worth two.
> —TALMUD, MEGILLAH 18A

PHRASE *Wisdom walks through the door of silence.*

PRACTICE Unless the words you are about to speak are absolutely necessary, remain silent.

JOURNAL

SILENCE

IF YOU FIND YOURSELF in company, it is better that you be told: "Speak, why are you so still?" Rather than that you speak and your words be burdensome to them and they will tell you: "Be quiet."

—*ORCHOT TZADDIKIM* (1540)

PHRASE   *Wisdom walks through the door of silence.*

PRACTICE   Unless the words you are about to speak are absolutely necessary, remain silent.

JOURNAL

IN SEEKING WISDOM, the first step is silence, the second listening, the third remembering, the fourth practicing, the fifth teaching others.

—RABBI SHLOMO IBN GABIROL (1021–1058)

PHRASE *Wisdom walks through the door of silence.*

PRACTICE Unless the words you are about to speak are absolutely necessary, remain silent.

JOURNAL

SILENCE

IF YOU CAN'T CONTROL yourself from feeling angry, at least you can keep silent. Then the anger will be barren and bear no fruit (of insults, disputes, and the like). This will also quiet the feelings of anger, since silence to anger is like water to fire.

—RABBI ELIEZER PAPO (1785–1826)

PHRASE *Wisdom walks through the door of silence.*

PRACTICE Unless the words you are about to speak are absolutely necessary, remain silent.

JOURNAL

BEFORE YOU OPEN your mouth, be silent and reflect: "What benefit will my speech bring me or others?"

—RABBI MENACHEM MENDEL LEFFIN (1749–1826)

PHRASE *Wisdom walks through the door of silence.*

PRACTICE Unless the words you are about to speak are absolutely necessary, remain silent.

——————— JOURNAL ———————

SILENCE

SAY LITTLE and do much.

—PIRKEI AVOT 1:15

PHRASE *Wisdom walks through the door of silence.*

PRACTICE Unless the words you are about to speak are absolutely necessary, remain silent.

———— JOURNAL ————

A TIME TO KEEP silent and a time to speak.

—ECCLESIASTES 3:12

PHRASE *Wisdom walks through the door of silence.*

PRACTICE Unless the words you are about to speak are absolutely necessary, remain silent.

——————— JOURNAL ———————

AWE

————

AWE IS A natural human response to an overwhelmingly profound experience. It takes no effort at all to feel the inner expansiveness that arises when our eyes take in a sunset or see a whale breaching. But only an inner instrument that has been polished and honed will find just as much awe in less dramatic situations—awe not because I see a sight, but because I am able to see, not because the sunset is spectacular, but because there is a sun. Cultivate the capacity to feel awe and the whole world becomes awesome.

> The beginning of wisdom is the awe of the Divine.
>
> —PROVERBS 1:7

PHRASE *The beginning of wisdom is awe.*

PRACTICE Wherever you may be, in the city or the country, indoors or outdoors, find moments to open yourself to experience the wonder of creation.

————— JOURNAL —————

TRUE AWE IS VERY difficult to attain. To the degree that one does attain it, however, it has the power to purify and sanctify.

—RABBI MOSHE CHAIM LUZZATTO (1707–1746)

PHRASE *The beginning of wisdom is awe.*

PRACTICE Wherever you may be, in the city or the country, indoors or outdoors, find moments to open yourself to experience the wonder of creation.

JOURNAL

AWE

AWE INSPIRED BY God's magnitude, exaltedness, and awesome power never leaves a person or parts from him all the days of his life. It is the gateway to pure love and intense yearning.

—RABBI BAHYA IBN PAQUDA (11TH CENTURY)

PHRASE *The beginning of wisdom is awe.*

PRACTICE Wherever you may be, in the city or the country, indoors or outdoors, find moments to open yourself to experience the wonder of creation.

JOURNAL

AWE AND LOVE are the two pillars of our divine service. One of these pillars, indeed, holds the key to all the facets of this service, and that is awe.

—RABBI ELIYAHU DE VIDAS (1518–1592)

PHRASE *The beginning of wisdom is awe.*

PRACTICE Wherever you may be, in the city or the country, indoors or outdoors, find moments to open yourself to experience the wonder of creation.

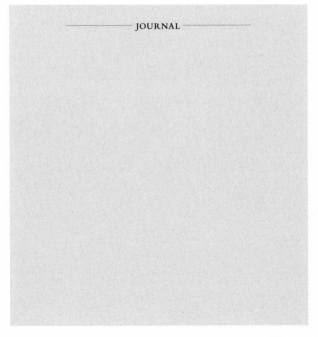

JOURNAL

AWE

To FEAR GOD is to be moved by a sense of awe, like that which one experiences in the presence of a great and awe-inspiring king. In every move that one makes, one ought to feel self-abased before the greatness of God. This is especially true when one addresses God in prayer, or engages in the study of God's Torah.

—RABBI MOSHE CHAIM LUZZATTO (1707–1746)

PHRASE *The beginning of wisdom is awe.*

PRACTICE Wherever you may be, in the city or the country, indoors or outdoors, find moments to open yourself to experience the wonder of creation.

———— JOURNAL ————

"ON THE HEEL OF HUMILITY comes awe of the Divine" (Proverbs 22:4). Humility will cause the awe of heaven to intensify in your heart.

—RABBI MOSES BEN NACHMAN, THE RAMBAM (1194–1270)

PHRASE *The beginning of wisdom is awe.*

PRACTICE Wherever you may be, in the city or the country, indoors or outdoors, find moments to open yourself to experience the wonder of creation.

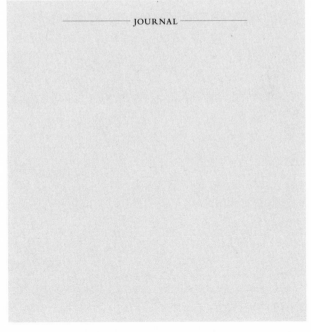

JOURNAL

AWE

"ALL IS IN THE HANDS of Heaven except for the awe of Heaven" (Talmud, Berachot 33b). Awe is generated from a person's deep awareness of the Creator and can only be instilled in a person if he chooses to instill it. We see from this that our awe of Heaven is dependent solely on us!

—RABBI ISSER ZALMAN MELTZER (1870–1953)

PHRASE *The beginning of wisdom is awe.*

PRACTICE Wherever you may be, in the city or the country, indoors or outdoors, find moments to open yourself to experience the wonder of creation.

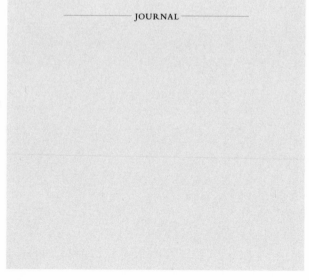

JOURNAL

Rava said, "When a person dies and is led in for his final judgment, he is asked, 'Did you deal with integrity, did you fix times for learning, did you engage in procreation, did you hope for salvation, did you engage in the dialectics of wisdom, did you understand one thing from another?' Yet even so, if the awe of the Lord is his treasure, it is well; if not, not."

—TALMUD, SHABBAT 31A

PHRASE *The beginning of wisdom is awe.*

PRACTICE Wherever you may be, in the city or the country, indoors or outdoors, find moments to open yourself to experience the wonder of creation.

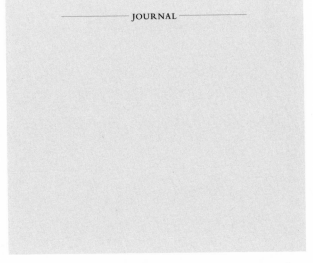

——— JOURNAL ———

Sources

The sources used for this book include the Torah, Mishna, Talmud, Midrash, and the following:

Ben Yechiel, Asher. *Orchot Chaim*. Translated by Yaakov Petroff. New York: Mesorah Publications, 1992.

Ben Yosef, Sa'adiah (Sa'adia Gaon). *The Book of Beliefs and Opinions*. Translated by Samuel Rosenblatt. New Haven, CT: Yale University Press, 1989.

Berezovsky, Shalom Noach (The Slonimer Rebbe). *Netivot Shalom*. Jerusalem: Yeshivat Beit Avraham Slonim, 1994.

Blazer, Yitzhak. "The Gates of Light." In *Ohr Yisrael*. New York: Targum/Feldheim Publishers, 2004.

Breuer, Salomon. *Chochmo U'Mussar*. New York: Feldheim Publishers, 1996.

Bunim, Irving M. *Ethics from Sinai*. New York: Feldheim Publishers, 2002.

Chasman, Yehuda Leib. *Ohr Yahel*. Jerusalem: 1972.

Cole, Peter, ed. and trans., *The Dream of the Poem: Hebrew Poetry from Muslim and Christian Spain*, 950–1492. Princeton, NJ: Princeton University Press, 2007.

Cordovero, Moshe. *Tomer Devorah* (*The Palm Tree of Deborah*). Translated by Moshe Miller. New York: Targum Press, 1993.

De Vidas, Eliyahu. *The Beginning of Wisdom: The Gate of Love*. Jersey City, NJ: Ktav Publishing, 2002.

Dessler, Eliyahu. *Michtav meEliyahu* (*Strive for Truth*). Edited by Rabbi Aryeh Carmell. New York: Feldheim Publishers, 1978.

Eliyahu of Vilna (The Vilna Gaon). *Even Shleimah*. New York: Mekhon ha'Gra, 1999.

Fendel, Zechariah. *The Ethical Personality*. New York: Hashkafah Publications, 1986.

Friedlander, Chaim. *Sifsei Chaim*. New York: Feldheim Publishers.

Gifter, Mordechai. *Pirkei Torah*. New York: Mesorah Publications, 1998.

Goldberg, Hillel. *Israel Salanter: Text, Structure, Idea*. Jersey City, NJ: Ktav, 1982.

———. *The Fire Within*. New York: Mesorah Publications, 1987.

Goldstein, David, trans., *The Jewish Poets of Spain*. New York: Penguin Publications, 1983.

Grodzinski, Avraham. *Toras Avraham*. Bene-Barak, Israel: Yeshivat Kotel Avrekhim, 1977–78.

Horowitz, Yeshayahu Segal. *Sh'nei Luchot ha'Brit*. Translated by Eliyahu Munk. Jerusalem: Urim Publications, 2000.

Hurwitz, Yosef Yozel (The Alter of Novarodok). *Madregat HaAdam*. Jerusalem: Yeshivat Ner Shemuel, 2002.

Hutner, Yitzchak. *Iggerot u-Ketuvim*. Brooklyn, NY: ha-Mosad Gur Aryeh, 1991.

Ibn Gabirol, Shlomo. *Mivchar haPeninim*. Tel Aviv: Sifriyat Po'alim ha-kibuts ha-artsi ha-Shomer ha-tsa'ir, 1976.

Ibn Paquda, Bachya. *Duties of the Heart*. Translated by Daniel Haberman. New York/Jerusalem: Feldheim Publishers, 1996.

Ickovitz, Chaim (of Vilozhin). *Ruach Chaim*. Jerusalem: Tushiyah, 1993.

Kagan, Israel Meyer (The Chofetz Chaim). *Chofetz Chaim: A Lesson a Day*. Translated and compiled by Shimon Finkelman and Yitzchak Berkowitz. Brooklyn, NY: Mesorah Publications, 1995.

Kaplan, Eliyahu Avraham. *B'Ikvot HaYir'ah*, second ed. Jerusalem: Mossad HaRav Kook, 1988.

Karelitz, Avrohom Yeshaya (The Chazon Ish). *Emunah uBitachon*. Translated by Yaakov Goldstein. Jerusalem: Am HaSefer, 2008.

Katz, Dov. *Tenu'at haMussar (The Musar Movement)*. Translated by Leonard Oschry. Tel Aviv: Orly Press, 1977.

Kook, Abraham Isaac. *Abraham Isaac Kook: The Lights of Penitence, The Moral Principles, Lights of Holiness, Essays, Letters, and Poems*. Translated by Ben Zion Bokser. New York: Paulist Press, 1978.

Krumbein, Elyakim. *Musar for Moderns*. New York: Ktav, 2005.

Leffin, Menachem Mendel. *Chesbon ha-Nefesh* [1845].

Translated by D. Landesman. New York: Feldheim Publishers, 1995.

Leibowitz, A. Henach. *Pinnacle of Creation*. New York: Mesorah Publications, 2007.

Levenstein, Yechezkel. *Ohr Yechezkel*. Monsey, NY: M. Shain, 1988.

Levovitz, Yerucham. *Daat, Chochmah U'Mussar*. Brooklyn, NY: Daas Chochmah U'mussar Publications, 1972.

Loew, Yehudah (The Maharal). *Netivot Olam*. Translated and adapted by Eliakim Willner. Brooklyn, NY: Mesorah Publications, 1994.

Lopian, Elya. *Lev Eliyahu*. Jerusalem: Ha'Va'ad l'Hotsa'at Kitve Maran, z"l, 1983.

Luzzatto, Moshe Chaim. *The Complete Mesillat Yesharim (The Path of the Just)*. Translated by Avraham Shoshana. Cleveland, OH: Ofeq Institute, 2007.

Maimon, Avraham (The son of Maimonides). *The Guide to Serving God*. Translated by Yaakov Wincelberg. New York: Feldheim Publishers, 2008.

Miller, Mordechai. *The Sabbath Shiur*. Gateshead-on-Tyne, England: Gateshead Foundation for Torah, 1973.

Morgenstern, Menahem Mendel (The Kotzker). *The Sayings of Menahem Mendel of Kotzk*. Translated by Sincha Raz. Lanham, MD: Jason Aronson Publishers, 1995.

Pam, Abraham. *Atareh LaMelech*. Brooklyn, NY: 1993.

Papo, Eliezer. *Pele Yoetz*. New York: Sepher-Hermon Press, 1991.

Pliskin, Zelig. *Patience*. Brooklyn, NY: Shaar Press, 2001.

Sabba, Avrahama. *Tzeror haMor.* Translated by Eliyahu Monk. Jerusalem: Urim Publications, 2008.

Salanter, Yisrael. *Ohr Yisrael.* New York: Targum/Feldheim Publishers, 2004.

Sefer HaChinuch. Translated by Charles Wengrov. New York: Feldheim Publishers, 1989.

Shkop, Shimon. *Shaarei Yosher.* New York: 1958.

Shmulevitz, Chaim. *Sichos Mussar.* New York: Artscroll, 1989.

Shraga Silverstein, trans., *Orchot Tzaddikim (The Ways of the Tzaddikim).* New York: Feldheim Publishers, 1995.

Wallach, Shalom Meir. *The Haggadah of the Mussar Masters.* New York: Artscroll, 1989.

Wolbe, Shlomo. *Alei Shur.* Jerusalem: Beit Ha'Mussar, 1986.

Yonah of Gerondi. *Commentary on Pirkei Avot.* Translated by David Sedley. Brooklyn, NY: Judaica Press, 2007.

Zaitchik, Chaim Ephraim. *Sparks of Mussar.* New York: Feldheim Publishers, 1985.

Ziv, Simcha Zissel (The Alter of Kelm). *Chochmah uMussar.* New York: Ateret Roshanu, 2000.

About the Author

ALAN MORINIS is an active interpreter of the teachings and practices of the Mussar tradition and regularly gives lectures and workshops. Born and raised in a culturally Jewish but nonobservant home, he studied anthropology at Oxford University on a Rhodes Scholarship, earning his doctorate at that university.

Alan has written books and produced feature films, television dramas, and documentaries, and has taught at several universities. The nearly lost Jewish spiritual discipline of Mussar has become his passion. He has been a student of the tradition since 1997, training under Rabbi Yechiel Yitzchok Perr, and he recorded his journey in the book *Climbing Jacob's Ladder* (Trumpeter, 2007). His guide to Mussar practice, *Everyday Holiness: The Jewish Spiritual Path of Mussar,* was also published by Trumpeter Books in 2007. He lives in Vancouver, British Columbia, with his wife of over thirty-five years, Dr. Bev Spring, and is the father of Julia and Leora.

About The Mussar Institute

THE MUSSAR INSTITUTE provides spiritual seekers with tools derived from and consistent with the classical Mussar tradition, to lift personal barriers to sanctity, in a practice supported by community and grounded in everyday life. It offers online courses, distance learning, local Mussar groups, practice support, national and regional gatherings, scholars, and guidance in personal practice.

To sign up for courses or learn more:
www.mussarinstitute.org
info@mussarinstitute.org

Alan Morinis, Founder